Strategies for Countering Non-State Actors in South Asia

Strategies for Countering Non-State Actors in South Asia

Edited by
Major General PJS Sandhu (Retd)

(Established 1870)

United Service Institution of India (USI)

Vij Books India Pvt Ltd
New Delhi (India)

Published by

Vij Books India Pvt Ltd
(Publishers, Distributors and Importers)
2/19 (Second Floor), Ansari Road, Darya Ganj
New Delhi-110002 (India)
Phone : +91-11- 43596460, +91-11- 65449971
Fax   :   +91-11- 47340674
web : www.vijbooks.com
Email: vijbooks@rediffmail.com

Copyright © 2011, United Service Institution of India, New Delhi

ISBN : 978-93-80177-62-5

CONTENTS

Concept Note

The current paradigm of violence in South Asia is based on militancy and strategic terrorism drawing from extremist ideologies, be it religion, ethnicity or sub nationalism across the region. While frequently fundamentalism is said to be the core of conflict in South Asia, there are many diverse threads to instability. The arc of insecurity and intensity of violence is extending each day, manifesting in different forms, be it Mumbai 26/11, Lahore 3/3, Marriott bomb attacks or air borne suicide strike in the heart of the capital Colombo.

The root of the problem in the region remains primacy of the non state vis a vis the state, be it in Swat in Pakistan, Helmand in Afghanistan or Abujmadh in India. The state has surrendered legitimacy due to poor institutional structures of governance and lack of will to enforce authority. More over non state actors are either left uncontrolled or being deliberately used by states as a strategic tool to create instability in the neighbourhood. Frequently this issue is seen from the perspective of combating terrorism, however, countering non state actors needs a focused approach by states in the region to address the challenges faced jointly by establishing mechanisms, strategies and tactics.

The aim of this Seminar is to examine the overall threat emanating from non state actors in South Asia, with particular reference to India and suggest a joint framework to neutralise the same. The study will examine contemporary and future security environment in South Asia and examine the threats and challenges. The phenomenon of Non State actors will be examined in detail to include armed Groups as Al-Qaeda, Lashkar e Tayyaba, Jaish e Mohammed, as well as Naxalites in the hinterland. Each facet of these to include Leadership Structure, Organisation, Political, Military, Judicial functions, Religious, Funding, Charity and aid arm, Media and Networking with other non state actors will be covered in detail.

Participants

Lieutenant General PK Singh, PVSM, AVSM, former General Officer Commanding-in-Chief South Western Command and Colonel Commandant, Regiment of Artillery, is an alumnus of the National Defence Academy and was commissioned into 2 Field Regiment (SP) Artillery on 16 December 1967.

During a military career spanning 41 years he has seen active service in the Western, Northern and North Eastern theatres including the 1971 Indo-Pak War.

A graduate of the Defence Services Staff College, Wellington and the National Defence College, New Delhi, his assignments include command of 101 Field Regiment (SP); a Mountain Brigade in active counter-insurgency operation in Nagaland / Manipur where he was awarded the Ati Vishisht Seva Medal; an Infantry Division (RAPID) during Operation Parakram and a Corps in the Western Theatre. After command of the Corps he was appointed Director General Operational Logistics at the Army Headquarters.

He has been a member of the Faculty at the Defence Service Staff College, Wellington; the Indian Military Academy, Dehradun; the School of Artillery, Devlali and the Computer Technology Wing of the Military College of Telecommunication Engineering, Mhow. During Operation Vijay he was Deputy Director General, MI (Foreign Division) at the Army Headquarters and was instrumental in shaping the contours of military diplomacy.

Admiral Vijai Singh Shekhawat, PVSM, AVSM, VrC, ADC grew up in a military environment having spent his childhood years in various cantonments including Peshawar and Dhaka in undivided India. His father , a paratrooper, was amongst the first officers to be commissioned from the Indian military Academy, Dehradun at its inception, into the Maratha Light infantry. Passing through several schools as the family moved on transfers, his main education was in Colonel Brown's school and St Joseph's Academy in Dehradun, Bishop Cotton Boys' school in Bangalore and St Joseph's College, North Point, Darjeeling.

His interest in the sea developed early from reading stories of sailing ships, pirates and far off Island, and joining the navy was almost a foregone conclusion. He was selected for the 7th Course of the Joint Services Wing, National Defence Academy, then at Clement Town, Dehradun, in January 1952. He was first in overall order of merit and awarded the President's gold Medal for the best all-round cadet on passing out in December, 1953.

During his Academy days, he was an outstanding sportsman and was awarded Blues in Athletics, Boxing, Football, Swimming and Riding. His early riding experience with the Mysore and the Gwalior Lancers stood him in good stead and he won the first prize in Cadet's Show Jumping at the frist post-war Army Horse Show held in New Delhi in 1954.He was a member of the academy debating teams participation in Inter-University debates, notably against Oxford University, and also a prominent member of the Dramatics.

Admiral Shekhawat has been a keen mountaineer having done the basic and advanced mountaineering courses from the Himalayan Mountaineering Institute, Darjeeling. He was a member of the successful Annapurna III (24, 858 feet) mountaineering expedition to Nepal in 1961 and has done extensive rock climbing in Wales, UK. His present active sporting interest is tennis.

After early sea training in frigates and cruisers as cadet and midshipman, he was commissioned on Ist July, 1956 and held various assignments in fleet ships before being sent to UK in 1959 for the new ASW Frigate Talwar as 2nd Gunnery Officer, and later, Navigating Officer on her return passage through the Mediterranean sea and the Suez Cannal.

A pioneer of the submarine arm, he did his basic submarine training in UK in 1963-64 and then in the USSR in 1966-67. He has been the Executive and Commanding Officer of several submarines,Commanded the submarine base and the 8th Submarine squadron at Visakhapatnam and was Director of the Submarine arm in 1975-77. He commissioned the submarines Kalvari(1967) and Karanj(1969) in the Baltic sea and sailed them through the Atlantic Ocean and round the Cape of good Hope to India, the Suez Canal being closed after the Arab-Israel War of 1967.

He attended the US Naval War College, Newport, USA in 1977-78 and subsequently commanded the ASW Frigate Himgiri during 1981-82. He was awarded the Vir Chakra for gallantry in commandof the submarine Karanj during the 1971 Indo-Pak War, the Ati Vishisht Seva Medal for distinguished service in 1984 and the Param Vishisht Seva Medal in 1991 for exceptional services.

Admiral VS Shekhawat has had close association with the training of junior officers. He was instructor on board the cadet and midshipmen training ships in 1957-59 and also at the National Defence Academy, Khadakwasla in 1961-63. He again served at the National Defence Academy in 1979-81 as Chicf Instructor and Deputy Commandant.

On promotion to Flag Rank in June, 1984, he served as assistant Chief of Naval Staff (operations) at Naval Headquarters. He commanded the prestigious Western Fleet, the strike force of the

Indian Navy, in 1986-87, coinciding with the period of operation Brasstacks, and was Flag Officer Commanding Maharashtra Area responsible for local Naval Defence forces in Naval Headquarter by 1987-88. Promoted Vice Admiral in Aug 1988 he was Director General of the tri-service Defence Planning Staff until Aug 1990.

From Dec 1990 to Oct 1992, Admiral Shekhawat was Flag officer Commanding-in-Chief Eastern Naval Command, with maritime defence responsibilities for the entire eastern seaboard and the Andman & Nicobar island. From Nov 1992 to Sep 1993, he was the Vice Chief of the Naval Staff and assumed the appointment of the Chief of the Naval Staff on 01 Oct 1993.

His long years at sea have taken him to most countries of the Indian Ocean littoral and he is deeply interested in the economic and maritime developments in the region. Extensive reading and travel in South East Asia, East and West Africa, the Far East, the Arab countries, the erstwhile Soviet Union, Europe and the USA have given him a keen insight in to global geostrategic issues.

Lieutenant General Vinayak Patankar (Retd), is an alumnus of the National Defence Academy. On graduation from the Indian Military Academy, he was commissioned in 17 Parachute Field Regiment in 1965.

General Patankar is a paratrooper and helicopter pilot. He is also a qualified flying instructor. He has had the privilege of participating in the 1965, 1971 and 1999 (Kargil) wars. He has received many honours and awards. He earned commendation of the Chief of Air Staff for handling a grave emergency while piloting a helicopter in 1976. He is also the recipient of Param Vishisht Seva Medal for his outstanding services to the Nation.

General Patankar has been trained at many military institutions in India and abroad, some of the important institutions being: -

(a)   Defence Services Staff College, Wellington.

(b)   Joint Services Staff College at Canberra, Australia.

(c)   Higher Command course at College of Combat (now Army War College), Mhow.

(d)   United States Army War College, at Carlisle, Pennsylvania, USA.

(e)   He also has a Master's Degree in Defence Studies from Madras University.

Command Assignments . He commanded 17 Parachute Field Regiment and later 59 Mountain Brigade engaged in counter insurgency operations in Manipur. During the Kargil war, he was commanding 28 Infantry Division on the Line of Control in J&K. For the role played by him in that war, he was awarded Uttam Yudh Seva Medal. Later he was the Corps Commander of the prestigious 15 Corps engaged in management of the Line of Control and counter terrorist operations in the Kashmir Valley.

Staff Assignments. General Patankar has served in various staff and instructional appointments. Some of the important ones among them were Brigade Major of an Infantry Brigade in Kashmir, Director at Military Operations Directorate, Army Headquarters, Instructor at the Defence Services Staff College, Deputy Director General (Strategic Planning) and later as Additional Director General, Perspective Planning at the Army Headquarters. He was the Quartermaster General of the Indian Army before he retired.

After retirement, Lt Gen Patankar has been associated with many think tanks in India and abroad as shown below: -

(a)   Distinguished Fellow at Observer Research Foundation, New Delhi.

(b)   Member, International Institute for Strategic Studies, London.

(c)   Member, Institute for Defence Studies and Analyses, New Delhi.

(d)   Member, United Services Institute, New Delhi.

(e)   Member, Centre for Land Warfare Studies, Delhi Cantt.

(f)   Member, Institute of Peace and Conflict Studies, New Delhi.

(g)   Member, Centre for Air Power Studies, Delhi Cantt.

He has not only contributed many articles to leading journals and news papers but has also authored the Army Aviation Doctrine published recently. He is the army editor of the magazine, India Strategic. He has been invited frequently to speak as well as to participate in seminars, conferences and panel discussions at many a prestigious forum within India and abroad. He has been interviewed by the BBC World TV in London, GEO TV in Dubai and participates fairly regularly on NDTV, CNN-IBN and CNBC.

Dr N. Manoharan is currently Senior Research Fellow at the Centre for Land Warfare Studies, New Delhi. He did his MPhil and Phd on South Asia from the School of International Studies, Jawaharlal Nehru University. He has over 15 years of research experience. He was South Asia Visiting Fellow at the East-West Center Washington (2005) and recipient of prestigious Mahbub-ul Haq Award (2006). His areas of interest include national security, terrorism, Sri Lanka, Maldives, human rights, ethnic conflicts, multiculturalism, security sector reforms and conflict resolution. His recent publications include *India's War on Terror* (New Delhi: Knowledge World, 2010), *SAARC: Towards Greater Connectivity* (New Delhi: Shipra, 2008); *Ethnic Violence and Human Rights in Sri Lanka* (New Delhi: Samskriti, 2007); *Counterterrorism Legislation in Sri Lanka: Evaluating Efficacy* (Washington D.C.: East-West Center, 2006). His forthcoming books are *Counter-terror Laws and Security in Developing Democracies: Lessons from India and Sri Lanka*, and *Sri Lanka: A Conflict Dictionary* (New Delhi: Routledge). He is currently working on 'Comprehensive Internal Security Strategy for India'.

Maj Gen GD Bakshi (Retd) is a combat veteran of many skirmishes on the LC and Counter-Terrorist operations in J&K and Punjab. He commanded his battalion in active operations in Kargil and was awarded the Vishist Seva Medal. Later he commanded a brigade in Counter-Terrorist operations in the very rugged mountains of Kishtwar and was awarded the Sena Medal for his distinguished services. He subsequently commanded the reputed Romeo Force during intensive Counter-Terrorist operations in the Rajouri-Punch Districts of J&K and succeeded in pacifying the area. He has served two tenures at the highly prestigious Directorate General of Military Operations and was the first BGS (IW) at HQ Northern Command where he dealt with Information Warfare and Psychological Operations. He is a prolific writer on matters military and non-military and has published 16 books and over 50 papers in many prestigious research journals. His articles have also been published in various National Newspapers. He taught at the Indian Military Academy, Dehradun and the Prestigious Defence Services Staff Collage at Wellington for three years each. He holds a Masters degree in Defence Science and an M Phil in Strategic Studies from the University of Madras. He is an Associate member of the IDSA. He taught at the National Defense College at

New Delhi for two years and retired from this prestigious assignment in Jun 08. He is a Strategic Analyst and has been contracted by the Army HQ and Integrated Defense Staff to carry out Net Assessments of Key Security issues. Concurrently he is also doing his Ph.D. (Limited Wars in South Asia) from the University of Madras. His books include, "Afghanistan-the First Fault line War," "War in the 21st Century", "The Indian Art Of War" " The Military Threat from Pakistan" etc.

Maj Gen Y K Gera (Retd). He was commissioned in the Corps of signals in 1957. He retired in Apr 1993 as Chief Signal Officer, Central Command, Lucknow.

During his career, Maj Gen YK Gera commanded a Corps Signal Regiment, served as Chief Signal Officer of a strike corps and Additional Director General of signals Intelligence.

Maj Gen YK Gera is a telecommunication Engineer, an associate member of the Institute of Engineers and a fellow of the Institute of Electronics and Telecommunication Engineers. He was a faculty Commander at the Military College of Telecommunication Engineering, Mhow.

A graduate from the Defence Services Staff College, Wellington, he has done the Long Defence Management Course from the College of Defence Management, Secunderabad and the National Security Management course from the National Defence University, Washington (USA). He is an alumnus of the National Defence College, New Delhi.

For three years after his retirement, Maj Gen Gera was on the panel of the Union Public Service Commission, New Delhi. He served as the Deputy Director and Editor of the United Service Institution of India (USI), New Delhi from 01 January 1997 to 30 April 2007. He functioned as the Chief Editor of the quarterly USI Journal dealing with national security and defence matters. His duties also involved overseeing research project studies by research scholars; interaction with foreign delegations, conduct of seminars and round table discussions pertaining to national security issues and defence matters.

Maj Gen YK Gera has travelled widely and has visited more than fifteen countries mostly as part of official delegations.

Shri Ajit Doval. A highly decorated IPS officer of Kerala Cadre, he retired as Director Intelligence Bureau in 2005. After topping Agra University in M.A. Economics in 1967, he joined Indian Police Service in 1968. He joined the Intelligence Bureau in 1972, and held various senior positions within the country and abroad including North-East, Sikkim, Punjab, J&K, Pakistan, U.K., etc. Highly rated expert on terrorism, counter-intelligence and operations, he was a Founder Chairman, Multi Agency Centre and Joint Task Force on Intelligence. He is a recipient of Kirti Chakra, one of the highest military decorations for Gallantry. He was also a country's youngest officer to be awarded prestigious Indian Police Medal for Meritorious Service at the age of 29 years, a record he still holds. A recipient of President's Police Medal for Distinguished Service, he is a graduate of National Defence College. A noted Strategic Analyst and writer on national security issues; he is presently Director Vivekananda Kendra International and Secretary General of Policy Perspective Foundation.

Shri Praveen Swami is associate editor of *The Hindu*, and also writes for its sister publication, *Frontline* magazine.

He reported on Jammu and Kashmir, Punjab, and security issues for much of the 1990s before becoming Mumbai bureau chief in 1998. Swami also served as a producer for an independent television network, where he worked on projects related to terrorism in Punjab.

He has won several awards for his work. He received the Sanskriti Samman award in 1999 for a series of investigative stories on Indian military and intelligence failures preceding and during the Kargil War. His work on the Indian Army's counterterrorist operations won him the Prem Bhatia Memorial Award for Political Journalism in 2003. In 2006, he also won the Indian Express-Ramnath Goenka Excellence in Journalism prize.

He was a Senior Fellow at the United States Institute of Peace in Washington, D.C. in 2004-2005.

Shri EN Rammohan, IPS (Retd) is 1965 Batch Assam Cadre, Indian Police Service officer. He retired from service as Director General of the Border Security Force in November 2000. After retirement, he has had a tenure as Advisor to the Governor of Manipur.

During his service, he served in Jorhat, Hojai, Sibsagar, Nowgong and Guwahati as Sub Divisional Police Officer (SDPO) and Addl SP and later as SP Shillong for two terms and then as DIG Northern Range in Tezpur during the elections of 1982-83. Later he was posted as JGP (Operations) during operation 'Bajrang' against ULFA insurgents in 1990. During this period he traveled extensively in all the 18 districts affected by the insurgency, interacted closely with the management of different Tea Gardens and with the Army in conducting operations. Subsequently, he was posted as IG CRPF, North East Region in Shillong and later moved as IG BSF Srinagar in June 1993.

He has extensive experience of combating insurgency. He has personal knowledge of the North East and has very close association with the people and the Police Forces. He has served in the state of Jammu and Kashmir as well as in the North East.

Vinita Priyedarshi. Currently pursuing her PhD from Jawaharlal Nehru University in International Politics, she possesses a gold medal in M.A. in political Science. She has worked as a Research Associate in institutions like CSDS (Centre for the Study of Developing Society) and IPCS (Institute for Peace and Conflict Studies) apart from assisting in Projects dealing with RTI and dementia. She has presented papers in various National Seminars on issues dealing with terrorism and insurgency. She is currently working as a Research Associate in USI-CS3.

She has published a number of articles in journals. Her most recent publication is on "Tracing the Tenets of Fourth Generation Warfare in Terrorist and Insurgent Organizations: The Case of Al-Qaeda" in April-June issue of India QUARTERLY. She has authored a book titled "Typology of Counter-terrorism Strategies: Comparative Study of India and Israel". Her area of interest includes terrorism, insurgency, nuclear issues and other aspects of internal security.

Admiral Madhvendra Singh assumed charge of the Indian Navy, as the 17th Chief of Naval Staff, on 29 December 2001. His father, the late Major General K. Bhagwati Singh (Retd.), was the first batch of Indian Cadets to pass out of the Indian Military Academy - along with Field Marshal SHFJ Manekshaw. The late Major General K.B. Singh (Retd.) has the distinction of having Indian Commission Number One.

After completing his schooling at the St. Xavier High School in Jaipur (Rajasthan), Madhvendra joined the National Defence Academy (NDA) at Khadakvasla in July 1958 and was commissioned into the Indian Navy on 01 January 1963. As a Cadet on board INS Krishna, he was awarded the Binocular for standing first in the overall Order of Merit and the Telescope for being the Best All Round Cadet. Later he was also awarded the coveted Sword of Honour on being adjudged the best all round Midshipman of the Fleet.

Admiral Singh specialised in Gunnery and has also undergone the Advanced Gunnery Course at the Royal Military College of Science at Shrivenham, United Kingdom. He is a Graduate of the Defence Services Staff College (DSSC), Wellington and a post-graduate of the Naval War College at Newport, USA and the National Defence College in New Delhi. He has commanded the aircraft carrier INS Viraat; the guided-missile destroyer INS Ranvir; the guided-missile frigate INS Talwar and the Naval Academy at Kochi.

Admiral Singh has also held important staff and training appointments, both afloat and ashore. As a Flag Officer, he has served as Chief of Staff of the Western Naval Command, the Chief Instructor (Navy) at the Defence Services Staff College (DSSC), Wellington and as the Flag Officer Commanding, Western Fleet, prior to taking over as the Assistant Chief of Naval Staff (Policy & Plans) at Naval HQ in June 1994. On promotion to Vice Admiral on 02 January 1995, he took over as the Controller of Warship Production & Acquisition (CWP&A) at Naval Headquarters and later took over as the Deputy Chief of Naval Staff (DCNS). He was appointed as the Flag Officer Commanding Southern Fleet on 23 October 1996 and took over as the Flag Officer Commanding-in-Chief, Western Naval Command on 31 March 1998. He was later appointed as the Vice Chief of Naval Staff (VCNS) in New Delhi on 03 April 2001.

The highlight of Admiral Singh's tenure at Mumbai was the successful conduct of the International Fleet Review (IFR) in February 2001 in which 70 Indian Navy and 30 foreign naval ships were reviewed by the then incumbent President of India K.R. Narayanan in Mumbai harbour. The prestigious event was attended by the then serving CNS, Admiral Sushil Kumar and senior naval officers from 30 other countries. He has twice been commended by the CNS and is a recipient of the Param Vishist Seva Medal (PVSM) and the Ati Vishist Seva Medal (AVSM) for distinguished service of a very high order. He took part in the liberation of Goa in December 1961 and in maritime operations in 1965 and 1971, as also in Operation Pawan in Sri Lanka in 1987. During the Kargil War in 1999, he was commanding the Western Maritime Theatre.

Admiral Singh is very fond of the outdoors and enjoys golf, yachting, riding and skeet shooting. An enthusiastic environmentalist, he is keen on preserving our maritime heritage and history. The Admiral is married to Mrs Kaumudi Kumari and they have a son, a daughter and a grandson. Mrs. Kumari is a special educator and has worked in schools run by the Spastic Society of India. Upon his retirement on 31 July 2004, he completed more than 41 years of distinguished service to the nation and to the Indian Navy.

Strategies for Countering Non-State Actors in South Asia

Inaugural Session

Welcome Remarks :   Lt Gen P K Singh,
PVSM, AVSM (Retd),
Director USI

Keynote Address :   Lt Gen CKS Sabu,
PVSM,AVSM,VSM
GOC-in-C South
Western Command

Inaugural Address :   Admiral V S Shekhawat,
PVSM, AVSM, VrC
(Retd)

Welcome Remarks

❏ **Lieutenant General PK Singh,PVSM,AVSM (Retd)**
   Director, USI

Distinguished members of the panel, General Officers, the Head of the Armed Forces Tribunal of the Jaipur Bench, officers of the Command Headquarter, ladies and gentlemen, there could not have been a happy occasion than this for me to be here back in Jaipur and to be given a chance to be participating in a seminar here. I must thank Gen. Sabu who has not only sponsored this study by a generous grant given to the USI, without which this study would not have been possible, but even organised the seminar in Jaipur. I am also thankful to the panelists who braved the heat and decided to come to Jaipur to be able to interact with us on a subject which is of great relevance to us.

The USI for those who don't know is a totally autonomous institution which dates back 140 years. We get no funds from the Government of India, we get no fund from the Services, we are a self supporting totally autonomous institution. We do everything with the help of the Army, Navy and Air Force which sponsors studies, who also give some of the officers on study leave to be as scholars and provide help to us. The USI was formed in 1870 and it became a registered society in 1874, making us one of the oldest registered societies of the country. The aim was to help service officers of those days understand and to get a global view of what is happening around the world for the British officers. The aim was not to tell them about India or about the Indian armed forces but to keep them aware of what is happening around the globe. They did that by having seminars like this which used to be invariably attended by the Commander-in-Chief and many of them were chaired by the then Viceroy and later even the Governor General. That is the importance Britishers gave to educating or keeping the officers updated on matters of interest to the British empire. They also reached out and held talks like this and seminars like this across the country. They wanted to reach out to wherever the officer community of the British rulers were.

I thank the Army Commander who agreed to hold this seminar in Jaipur, where we can interact with people and put across our views. We have an eminent panel, people who are experts in their fields, people who write, who think, who deliberate on these subjects and they have very kindly agreed to present their views here, but more importantly we have kept enough time for interaction and they have been kind enough to accept questions from you not just on the subject but also in their domain of specialisation. We have people like Mr Ram Mohan, all of you must have read his name, he was the DG BSF, he was at the Dantewada Enquiry Commission, he has tremendous experience. We have Mr Doval who retired as the Director of the Intelligence Bureau and now heads one of the most important think tank which has been set up in Delhi. Similarly we have Gen. Patankar, we have people who are experts, we have an eminent journalist, so please do not hesitate to reach out and ask them what you like but more importantly I have a very young lady who is a scholar in my institution who is a brave girl to be studying subjects like 4th Generation Warfare, who is writing a paper on that, who is looking at internal security, she needs the encouragement and of course she needs to answer your questions. So, we are trying to build up the next generation of thinkers, the next generation of scholars who will look at matters of national security.

The last thing I would like to say is, you the serving fraternity must put across what you want the research institution to be looking at, what is it that you want them to be looking at, what are your ideas on the subject, I think the time has come to bridge the gap between those who are doing thinking and writing and those who are executing it. Everywhere else in the world officers take part in international seminars, they rub shoulders with officers from other countries, they rub shoulders with scholars from other countries and they contribute. I think you will be doing us a great service by questioning us and giving us your ideas on the papers which we are writing now. They will not be the end product, they get further refined and take your views into account so that it enriches our knowledge, it enriches the final product that we will make. I would once again like to thank the Army Commander and each one of you for being here. It will be a biggest encouragement for us in our study if we are able to take away something from you today. Once again thank you very much for supporting the USI and supporting us in our endeavors.

Thank you very much and I will now request the Army Commander to say a few words.

Key Note Address

❏   Lt Gen CKS Sabu, PVSM,AVSM,VSM

It gives me immense pleasure this morning in welcoming you all to this Seminar on 'Strategies for Countering the Non State Actors in South Asia'. The seminar is organized under the aegis of USI and on my request being held in Jaipur, so that the formation commanders and officers from South West Command could attend this and benefit. Accordingly, it was clubbed with the Formation Commanders conference. At the outset I would like to extend a very warm welcome to Lt. Gen. PK Singh, Director, USI, and a former GOC-in-C of South Western Command, from whom I had the privilege of taking over the command. It is also my very pleasant duty to extend a very warm welcome to Admiral Shekhawat, Admiral Madhvendra Singh, then of course we have Justice Bhamru Khan, Gen. Sushil Gupta, the TT members, Gen Patankar and all the other distinguished speakers and guests for this seminar.

The subject of this seminar has importance and is relevant to every nation today perhaps, and nations may neglect this aspect only at their peril. I think no nation has suffered more from terrorism than India and since 1990 India has been plagued by what is termed as terrorism, which is today global, it is amorphous, it is lethal, and above all it is being prosecuted by a group of people who are highly motivated. In South Asia's very volatile geopolitical scenario with political unrest, which is rampant in some of India's immediate neighbouring countries, it is not enough for us to guard against conventional military threats across borders. India also needs to put together an urgent plan to deal with the Non State Actors, which has emerged as a very potent threat to our security. In the recent past India has witnessed more terrorist incidents than any other nation in the world. It is therefore pertinent for us to examine the rise of terrorism and the form and shape it has taken today in South Asia and world wide, and the threat that it poses to us today.

9/11 really highlighted the qualitative transformation in the security challenges in the international affairs and arena i.e. terrorism. Although guerrillas were waging revolutionary warfare using the terrorist tactics, contemporary escalation of this terrorism that we see today in the international system has been utilized mostly by the Non State Actors. Terrorism has assumed a transnational or a stateless form, in that it has neither a particular home country that it seeks to liberate nor a homeland to be used as a base for operations. 9/11 amongst other things highlighted beyond doubt that even a powerful nation like the US was helpless against such attacks. In our own case the Mumbai attack in a similar manner highlighted the helplessness of the Indian nation when 10 men really held to ransom the entire nation for 96 hours. These two incidents very clearly highlight some of the issues that have relevance today to us.

Firstly, from a security perspective the most disturbing aspect of 9/11 or 26/11 was not the horrible destruction, loss of life and property and the trauma of the terror, but the fact that the attackers did not at any time even factored the opposition of the US military or the Indian military. They did not do it in their planning nor their execution. These are militaries which are modern and who spend trillions and billions of dollars respectively to ensure that they are operationally ready to defend their country. In the hour of crisis we found that they were not acting as a deterrent which is what was required of them. The real threat is the rapid rise of the global terrorism over the last decade is a fact that another state but rather the super empowered group has taken. The rise of such empowered group is a trend that puts powerful technological tools and knowledge in the ever increasing sense. These groups using the leverages provided by these latest technologies are posing an entirely different threat, enter the non state actors and the fourth generation warfare. Technology today is advancing on a broad front and there are no barriers to it. The recent example if I may quote one is Japan's realization that the Sony Playstation console has the sufficient strengths and capabilities to be used to pilot a missile on a designated target. Also with the advances in genetics, engineering, and nano-technology, some of the many potential future threats that are emerging, we come closer to a point when a single individual will have the wherewithal namely the knowledge, the tools and the budget necessary to mount such an attack in the future.

As far as innovation of ideas is concerned, the non State enemy has also leveraged very effectively the vast literature that is available on guerilla warfare, in particular the concept of fourth generation warfare which has been developed and put to effectively. While the image of an Al Qaeda strategist sitting in an Afghanistan cave gleaning over the concepts of fourth generation warfare may not be something really that we can visualize but surely it has happened. 9/11 is the first application of fourth generation warfare by an autonomous non-state group not acting as a proxy for a foreign power. There is another major lesson that has been learnt by the prosecutors of the fourth generation warfare, and that is, an attack on the system can magnify the effects of a small scale attack into a major economic catastrophe. It has been computed that the Al Qaeda attack on WTC would have cost approximately about 250,000 dollars to mount the whole attack from planning to execution, which has resulted in a loss of the US to the tune of 80 billion dollars. That is a conservative estimates. By some estimates it is pegged at 500 billion dollars as an Immediate loss. That is an order of magnification of 2 million times. This does not count the moral effect of the attack as indeed the cost of hundreds of billions of dollars that has been spent since then in mounting the global war on terror.

The exponential magnitude of losses enabled by a system disruption which is what it was in addition to the moral and the resultant effect the cumulative effect would be long term, endless and resulting in huge damages and costs in billions of dollars. This could drag even a superpower amongst our nations into very serious and dire trouble. Systempunk is a new coined word which actually defines system disruption. In the same league as Shuapunk, systempunk is hitting back the system and destablising it with cascading effects which is going to bring to its knees the nation and the critical areas that are required to be protected, if a nation has to function. The Soviet Union imploded because of a system disruption which was crafted over three decades or more. A similar small groups carrying out such attacks on vital installations can really bring down nations and disrupt their functioning on a day to day basis.

I think there is a need therefore, when we view the situation in South Asia, it is quite grim. There have been several developments in recent years that do not augur well for the region. Firstly, the region has become a battleground for international terrorism led by Al Qaeda. Second, there are numerous religious groups which are strongly influenced by Al Qaeda and are waging war within their own State. The Taliban in Afghanistan, Pakistani Taliban, the Lashkar-e-Toiba of Taliban, HUJI in Bangladesh, LTTE in Sri Lanka, and many other terrorist organizations within the countries of the neighbouring region also continue to receive support and cooperation from these actors. Thirdly, within each state there are numerous non state actors and terrorist organizations which have been fighting the state, causing loss of life in addition to damage the State property. Terrorist organizations are calibrating such attacks which are more lethal than ever before, with a constant fear of your success and gaining access finally to weapons of mass destruction, including chemical and biological weapons from sources outside the region. Finally, terrorism in South Asia has the potential to destroy relations between countries, bringing them to the brink of war. Terrorism continues to be the biggest scourge that afflicts development of South Asia. Cross border terrorism has the potential to finally configurate into a conflict between nations.

In conclusion, gentlemen, what I wish to say is that there is an urgent need for a regional strategy and cooperation in South Asia which I am sure will emerge during the discourse that is going to take place in the three sessions we have this morning and afternoon and more needs to be done to build and support institutional framework at the regional level to promote these values rather than continuing to place too much emphasis on military approaches which will only lead to chaos. A viable counter terrorism strategy, therefore, should not only concentrate on stopping violence, but must question and condemn the irrational ideologies that undermine the development of healthy democratic institutions and good governance. We have in our midst today some of the brightest and most experienced analysts who have made a mark in their respective fields. It is a rare opportunity for all of us attending this seminar to understand this problem with greater clarity if I may say and learn from the collective wisdom of the distinguished speakers who are going to appear before you today. Thank you.

Inaugural Address

❏   **Admiral VS Shekhawat**

"Battle for the Mind and Matters of Governance"

Terrorism of various hues occupies increasing space in the consciousness of civil society and security experts. There is no commonly accepted definition. One man's terrorist is another's freedom fighter. To imperial colonizers anyone who resisted was a terrorist; to the colonized sufferers, they were their heroes fighting for independence. The most famous recent example of terrorist turned freedom fighter and revered world statesman is Nelson Mandela. It is evident that there is considerable subjectivity in defining terrorism.

"Violent activity or intent calculated to intimidate a society or government to further political, ideological or religious aims", could be taken as one simplified definition of terrorism. Violence by one state against another is normally an act of war, which could invite a riposte. But some states get away by violence through covert, deniable means, deploying or enabling Non State Actors (NSAs), that is individuals or groups enjoying the support or indulgence of the state.

Less commonly, there may be individuals with private agendas working contrary to the interest of their host state. Or to use terms introduced by B. Raman, a perceptive security analyst, "self motivated" and "freelance jihadists" as in some recent incidents. The permutations and combinations are many and complex.

Discussion on international terrorism invariably leads to Pakistan, a country which even its friends now acknowledge as the inspirational source of most terror incidents in the west. When it comes to terrorism against India however, disapprobation of Pakistan is muted by their dependence on its cooperation in Afghanistan; and the fact that it has been an ally of the west for over 60 years and also has the support of China and many Arab countries.

Pakistan depicts Kashmir as the root cause of its differences with India and presents its claims to it as the chief reason for supporting so-called "freedom fighters", now increasingly surplus Pashtuns from its jihad camps. Setting aside legalities, Kashmir is indeed a most difficult issue, made more complex by western manipulation since partition and the Cold War, encouraging unrealistic expectations in Pakistan and enabling myth making to rewrite history through propaganda, school text books, *madrassa* indoctrination and the like.

Pakistan was founded as a theological state and it was logical that the clerics would become steadily more assertive, culminating in rigid, doctrinaire Islam under Zia-ul-Haq. Pakistan encouraged Arabisation and Wahabisation of moderate religious practices of sub-continental Islam to obtain Saudi financial largesse. In the battle for the mind of its citizens it has single mindedly nurtured a belief system of distinctiveness from India in order to justify partition and therefore its own separate existence.

Pakistani history and school text books foster many myths for example that Pakistan was always a Muslim land and India was carved out of it! School children are taught rhymes describing Indians as dogs. The mosques and the *madrassas* complement what the schools purvey. Rabble rousers patronized by the state freely spew hatred. Little wonder that the jihad factories do not lack pliable material to further the hate agenda against India. Despite some positive signs, it is too early to interpret initiatives like *'aman ki asha'* by leading media groups of India and Pakistan. Only time will tell.

The torrent of aid and arms received from the USA, Saudi Arabia and China against the Soviets in Afghanistan whetted Pakistan's strategic ambitions even into central Asia, further boosted by American oil interests in Turkmenistan and the Caspian region. Despite the unravelling of its grand vision and the exposure of its role in jihadi violence following the destruction of the World Trade Centre on Sept. 11, 2001, it has skillfully parleyed its strategic location to sustain confrontation and a clandestine war against India using highly trained and motivated NSAs.

India will undoubtedly overcome the NSAs by appropriate action. What it cannot do is to dismantle the inspirational source and bring about a change in Pakistan's assiduously created belief system which is now Frankenstein-like, consuming its creators. It is doubtful if even Pakistan alone can change itself without pressure from its benefactors who have been complicit in nurturing its illusions over many years.

Of greater concern than foreign supported NSAs are homegrown groups such as the Naxalites, ULFA and others. Here the issues involved are rooted in history, with complex political, social, cultural, ethnic and religious dynamics. Many have festered for years, vested interests have developed in perpetuating the *status quo* and very often the original grievance is scarcely relevant. In almost every case there is a failure of the state, either by its absence, or an overbearing, exploitative presence. Missing, is the good governance and administration for which the state exists.

Somehow, the modern nation state does not like diversity and prefers homogeneity, at least in a social sense. The nomadic gypsies of Europe, tracing their ancient roots to India, are a persecuted lot, reviled as colourful rascals, increasingly unwelcome around their traditional camping grounds. The north American Indians have been confined to 'reservations', the Eskimos are no longer capable of hunting in their traditional ways due to dependence on snow mobiles which they often ride to a freezing death, unable to comprehend that fuel eventually runs out.

The Indian tribal or indigenous population has fared only marginally better. The Andaman and Nicobar, and other tribals are a vanishing breed under the civilizing mission of the state. Supposedly enlightened policies have not translated into commensurate benefits on the ground. Accustomed to living off the community assets of the forest they have had to contend with the demands of development, frequently an euphemism for expropriation of their traditional rights to the land, trees, forest produce, animals and water. With unimaginative development comes the paraphernalia of the state, the all-powerful and often corrupt BDO, the rapacious contractor, the distant and often indifferent Collector awaiting posting to the state capital. It is a fertile field for ideologues and activists, sometimes inspired from abroad such as the Maoists, to generate opposition and resistance to constitutional authority and in their turn, exploiting the simple tribal folk for their own ends; in essence, for political power.

Indigenous insurgencies are not entirely local, though they have local characteristics. Their origins go to the fundamentals of our political and administrative system as it has evolved: how our political parties function and are financed, how MPs and MLAs are elected, how governments are formed, how they govern or not, how they are accountable, what if they fail their electorate and so on. The rank and file of our bureaucracy and police forces are notorious for their indifference and inefficiencies, notwithstanding some outstanding and dedicated individuals. It is like a huge undisciplined army unlikely to win many battles and most assuredly losing the *civic* war. Without a deep and wide-ranging top down clean-up and reform of our political, civil service and police functioning we are unlikely to see a peaceful and constructive community with shared aspirations for a bright future. Knowledgeable persons speak of the despair in large parts of the countryside due to maladministration and natural causes like drought etc. Unrest is spreading in urban areas due to lack of planning vision, decaying infrastructure, crime, corruption and insensitivity at every level where the citizen encounters the state.

In a relatively peaceful city like Jaipur there are daily demonstrations against no electricity or water supply. This is not likely to improve in the foreseeable future – over many years governments have wantonly sold off public lands to malls and commercial enterprises, squeezing road and pedestrian space and have allowed land mafias to encroach on catchment areas of traditional *nalas, baoris,* depressions and reservoirs. No recharge of aquifers is taking place under the concrete jungles where once there were fields and forests. The state prefers to bring water from distant, depleting sources, possibly because there is big money to be made in major projects, little in unglamorous maintenance. Full page advertisements at public expense extol nebulous achievements of governments, with little to show on the ground, except sometimes, monuments to folly.

NSAs do not exist in a vacuum; they need a favourable environment, motivation, leadership, access to funds and weapons and some degree of support from the disaffected. They emerge from belief systems or ideologies which a state has enabled or tolerated. Incompetent and corrupt administrations ease their tasks and make countering them harder. But they can be overcome with good organization and well designed security responses as has been demonstrated many times, even in India.

The inspirational roots are harder to eradicate, nestling in the philosophical conception of the state; theological and exclusivist in Pakistan, secular and inclusive in India. From these derive the belief systems which in an amorphous way seep into the population and colour its thoughts and actions. In the case of indigenous movements, the noble words of the Constitution ring hollow under the burden of grinding poverty and vicious exploitation of the rural poor and the tribals. Only a revolution of good governance can assuage the anger of the doubly exploited and oppressed, both by the state and the NSAs.

Session – I

The Evolution of Non State Actors

Chairman   -   Lt Gen V G Patankar,
                             PVSM,UYSM,VSM
                             (Retd)

Speakers   -   Dr N Manoharan

                  -          Maj Gen G D Bakshi,
                             SM,VSM (Retd)

                  -          Maj Gen Y K Gera
                             (Retd)

Beyond Sovereignty
Contextualizing Violent Non-State Actors

N. Manoharan

Non-state actors (NSAs) are all those actors that are not (representatives of) states, yet operate and influence at both national and international levels. They could be violent or non-violent ("bad" or "good" in normal parlance).[1] Use of violence or force – "hard power" – is the basic distinction between the two. The focus of this paper is on violent/armed-NSAs which pose threat to state, human and global security. They not only trigger conflicts, but also pose immense resistance to conflict resolution. In short, violent NSAs (VNSAs) are groups that are armed and use violence to achieve their objectives. They are usually not under any state control, but may be supported by state actors in a formal or informal manner. Such support by states is extended for their asymmetrical warfare strategy in return for recognition, support and other benefits rendered to VNSAs. VNSAs range from rebel groups, irregular armed groups, insurgents, dissident armed forces, guerillas, liberation movements, terrorist organisations, bandits, criminal gangs to *de facto* territorial governing bodies. Some refer to these groups as "para-states", as they challenge state's monopoly of use of force.[2] With the emergence of VNSAs, nature of warfare itself has changed; a phenomenon known as 'Grey Area War' has emerged in which at least one antagonist in a conflict is a VNSA. The security environment of the

---

[1] Examples of "good" non-state actors are community-based organisations, women's groups, human rights associations, non-governmental organisations, religious organisations, farmers' cooperatives, trade unions, universities, research institutes, the media, the private sector, grassroots organisations, inf ormal private sector associations, etc.

[2] Phil Williams, "Violent Non-state Actors and National and I nternational Security," *International Relations and Security Network* , 2008, p. 4.

21st century, as a consequence, is set to be characterised by VNSAs.[3]

According to Federation of American Scientists, there are about 385 VNSAs world over.[4] As the State – termed as "impenetrable unit" – started losing its grip with the onset of globalisation, the VNSAs have been increasing in their power and influence and have added "immense uncertainty to already turbulent world security situation."[5] Numerous suitors have emerged – ranging from religion to ethnicity – competing with the State to gain individual's attention and loyalty. And the objectives of these suitors are at odds with States' goals.

Understanding VNSAs

Violent non-state actors can be understood in two broad contexts: historical and environmental.

Historically, VNSAs are not a new phenomenon. They are as old as the history of mankind. They have been part of conflicts for centuries. However, when Westphalian state system started consolidating in the 17th century the VNSAs remained insignificant at both domestic and international politics. They only emerged as part of decolonisation process in the early and mid 20th century. During the Cold War both Super Powers supported VNSAs as tools of 'proxy war' by dubbing them as "freedom fighters" principally in the Third World (Africa, Asia and Latin America).[6] The end of bipolarity in 1990 witnessed proliferation of VNSAs mainly because of the birth of several new but weak sovereign states. VNSAs, in fact, became

---

[3] See Max G. Man waring (ed.), *Gray Area Phenomena: Confronting the New World Disorder* (Boulder: Westview, 1993).

[4] For the comprehensive list of VNSAs, arranged in alphabetical order see http://www.fas.org/irp/world/para/index.html

[5] Troy S. Thomas, Stephen D. Kiser, and William D. Casebeer, *Warlords Rising: Confronting Violent Non-state Actors* (Lanham, MD: Lexington Books, 2005), p. xi.

[6] See Mohammed Ayoob (ed.), *Conflict and Intervention in the Third World* (London: Croom Helm, 1980).

prominent in the social science literature especially since the end of Cold War. The absence of Super Power rivalries made the VNSAs to look elsewhere for support. The end of Cold War also facilitated massive proliferation of small arms boosting the violence making capacity of VNSAs. The political, economic, social and technical trends of the early twenty first century not only encouraged the growth of armed groups but vastly increased their number, variety, power and impact in the international arena.[7] Post 9/11, the US-led 'Global War on Terror' cracked on all VNSAs by terming them as "terrorists". International norms that shielded VNSAs enjoying sanctuary in other countries took a beating. As a result, post-9/11 cross-border attacks targeting VNSAs increased as in US in Af-Pak region, Israel in Lebanon and Gaza, Ethiopia in Somalia, Turkey in Iraq etc.[8] Despite this, the overall intensity of violence caused by VNSAs world over has increased.

In the context of environment, the roles NSAs play, and the influence they exert, depend upon political, economic, and social context of the countries/environment they operate. By taking development as a yardstick, all States fall in any of the three broad categories: under-developed, developing and developed. While "bad" NSAs dominate under-developed states, "good" NSAs are abundant in developed countries; developing states have a mix of both. The violent NSAs are especially sophisticated in their exploitation of "grey areas" where states are weak, corruption is rampant, and the rule of law is nonexistent.[9] Data from the University of Maryland show that most VNSAs came from low-income authoritarian countries afflicted by conflict.[10] Weak states provide VNSAs safe havens, conflict experience, settings for training and indoctrination, access to

---

[7] Francis Fukuyama, *State-Building: Governance and World Order in the 21st Century* (Ithaca: Cornell University Press, 2004), p. 92. See also Hooman Peimani, " World Disorders: Troubled Peace in the Post-Cold War Era," *International Journal of Comparative Sociology*, Vol. 62, 2001.

[8] Ian Bry an, "Sovereignty and Foreign Fighter Problem," *Orbis*, Winter 2010, p. 125.

[9] David S ogge, "Repairing the W eakest Links: A New Agenda for Fra gile States," *Project Report*, FRIDE, October 2009, p. 5.

[10] For the comprehensive database see http://www.start.umd.edu/gtd/

weapons and equipment, financial resources, staging grounds and transit zones, targets for operations, and pools of recruits.[11]

Typology

All VNSAs fall under one of the following categories:

1. **Nationalistic:** Rebel groups that fight for the 'liberation' of, or an autonomy, or a separate state on behalf of a 'nation'. The agenda is ethno-nationalist or social-revolutionary. Such VNSAs see themselves as "future governors" and consciously prepare themselves for the future. They wear uniforms and display other symbols to project themselves as present combatants and "future armies"; their aim is to claim parity with the state forces in the eyes of the international law.[12] They usually follow guerilla warfare tactics, although conventional resistance is resorted on-and-off just to keep alive the aura of parity with the state. In this regard, popular support is their main strength using which they swim like fish in the sea of their ethnic constituency.[13] Moral, material and other support systems are also drawn from the same constituency. ETA of Spain, LTTE of Sri Lanka (till recently), IRA of United Kingdom, and PKK of Turkey are some of the rebel groups that fall in this category. They also often receive support from same ethnic groups but situated across the borders as the LTTE received from Tamil Nadu, IRA from Ireland and PKK from Kurds of Iraq.

2. **Ideological:** VNSAs belonging to this category are usually driven by Leftists or Rightist ideological motivations. The

---

[11] Sebastian Mallaby, "The Reluctant Imperialist: Terrorism, Failed States and the Case for American Empire,"*Foreign Affairs* 81, 2 (March/April 2002).

[12] Ulrich Schneckener, "Spoiler or Governance Actors? Engaging Armed Non-State Groups in Areas of Limited Statehood,"*SFB-Governance Working Paper Series*, No. 21, October 2009, p.9.

[13] This is a famous metaphor of Mao, quoted time and again in several counter-insurgency literature.

common mode of violence is terrorism to spread fear and panic among the people to achieve political ends, which usually are not territorial. They operate mostly in a clandestine manner in small groups. They target both civilian and military targets using kidnapping, indiscriminate bombings, hostage taking, hijacking, suicide attacks, assassinations, and sabotage.[14]

3. **Opportunistic:** VNSAs under this category range from criminal gangs, warlords, pirates, mercenaries, and mafia. They indulge in robbery, illegal trafficking, smuggling, piracy, gun running and contract killing purely for profit. They do not have any political or revolutionary aims and do not enjoy any popular support.[15] However, they often connive with terrorist and rebel groups for specific purposes.

However, this typology does not have clear cut boundaries. There are instances where some VNSAs fall simultaneously under two or all of the above categories. Similarly, there is a tendency of some VNSAs to slither from one category to another.

Rise & Growth

There are various reasons for the rise of NSAs. The prominent among them are failure of state actors in fulfilling their basic social contracts.

[14] Notable works on the subject include Jeff rey D. Simon, *The Terrorist Trap* (Bloomington: Indiana Univ ersity Press, 1994); Bruce Hoff man, *Inside Terrorism* (New Y ork: Columbia University Press, 2006); Walter Laqueur, "Postmodern Terrorism", *Foreign Affairs*, Vol. 75, No. 5, (1996), pp. 24-36; Ashton B. Carter , John Deutch & Phi lip Zelikow, "Catastrophic Terrorism", *Foreign Affairs*, Vol. 77, No. 6, (1999), pp . 80-94; David C. R apoport, "The Fourth Wa ve: September 11 and the History of T errorism," *Current History*, December 2001, pp. 419-24; Walter Laqueur, *The New Terrorism: Fanaticism and the Arms of Mass Destruction*, (London: Oxford University Pr ess, 1999; P aul R. Pil lar, "Terrorism Goes Glo-bal: Extremist Groups Extend Their Reach W orldwide," Brookings Institution, 23 February 2009; Ian Lesser et al, *Countering the New T errorism* (Santa Monica, CA: Rand, 1999; Andrew Tan & K umar Ramakrishna (eds.), *The New T errorism – Anatomy , Trends and Counter-Strategies*, (Singapore: Eastern Universities Press, 2002); Nadine Gurr & Ben-jamin Cole, *The New F ace of T errorism: Thr eats from Weapons of Mass Destruction* , (London: I.B. Tauris, 2000); Russell D. How ard & Reid L. Sla yer (eds.) *Terrorism and Counterterrorism – Understanding the New Security Environment* , (Guildford: McGraw-Hill, 2003).

[15] Klejda Mulaj (ed.), *Violent Non-state Actors in World Politics* (London: Hurst, 2009), p. 2.

There are three kinds of state failure: illegitimacy, incapacity, and coercion. States with low legitimacy and high in coercion are not in a position to sustain loyalty of their subjects. This applies even when a section of population is neglected or discriminated on the basis of ethnicity or any such category. Similarly, inability of states in addressing the problems of its citizens reinforces illegitimacy.[16] 'Protecto ergo obligo' ('I protect therefore I am obeyed'). In such circumstances, alternative affiliations tend to develop if even a section of population perceive that the state is no more an asset, but only a liability. In other words, the VNSAs grow because of weakness of states. The VNSAs seek to perpetuate and intensify this state weakness. For this, "identity entrepreneurs" help to "create" or "reinforce" the identity that now stands opposed to the state and seek to convert citizens into VNSA members.[17]

Various identity cleavages based on ethnicity, religion, class, etc are used to maintain group cohesion.[18] Consequently, the VNSAs in one degree or another seek to compensate for those shortcomings of the state and in a way justify their existence and command their support base. They challenge state's sovereignty in two ways: firstly, blocking state's ability to enforce its will, and secondly, by attempting to overthrow the sovereign itself.[19]

The non-state actors become particularly dangerous when they are hosted by or operate in conjunction with state actors for the purpose of asymmetric or proxy war strategies.[20] Apart from strategic

---

[16] Troy S. Thomas, Stephen D. Kiser, and William D. Casebeer, *Warlords Rising: Confronting Violent Non-state Actors* ( ), p. 55. Also see Robert I. R otberg (ed.), *State Failure and State Weakness in a Time of T error* (Cambridge, Mass.: W orld Peace Foundation, 2003).

[17] Jason Bartolomei, William Casebeer, "Troy Thomas, Modeling Violent Non-State Actors: A Summary of Concepts and Methods," Institute for Information Technology Applications Information Series No. 4, November 2004, p. 6.

[18] Thomas, n. 16, p. 63.

[19] See Hendrik Spruyt, *The Sovereign State and its Competitors: An Analysis of Systems of Change* (Princeton: Princeton University Press, 1996).

[20] For detailed treatment of the subject see Daniel Byman, *Deadly Connections: States that Sponsor Terrorism* (Cambridge: Cambridge Univ ersity Press, 2005).

aim of destabilizing neighbours using VNSAs, some states use VNSAs also as tools of power projection. The classic case is use of groups like Lashkar-e-Toiba (LeT) and Jaish-e-Muhammad (JeM) by Pakistan against India. Here Pakistan is a "base state" used as a base by VNSAs to launch attack against the "target state" India.

While having several positives, globalization also has many side effects. One of them was aiding proliferation and strengthening of VNSAs. Globalisation, apart from diluting state's sovereignty, has provided enough force multipliers and facilitators for VNSAs to strengthen themselves. Flow of arms, funds and other resources, travel and communications for the VNSAs have become easier than ever before.[21] As a result, it has become easier for the VNSAs to network and make alliances with like-minded groups to achieve common objectives. Al Qaeda, for instance, has made much use of forces of globalization in achieving its objectives.

Characteristics of VNSAs

Despite various typologies, present day VNSAs share certain common characteristics.

Global & Amorphous:

The globalised 'flat world'[22] has facilitated not only easy movement of VNSAs, but also their operations, support systems and methods. With advancements in information and communication technology VNSAs are now in a position to guide operations, thousands of kilometers away. World Wide Web is also used as a tool of propaganda and fundraising by these groups.[23] The organisational structure of modern day VNSAs is more networked than the

---

[21] John Mackinlay, "Globalisation and Insurgency,"Adelphi Paper 352 (London: The International Institute for Strategic Studies, 2002).

[22] For detailed exposition on the 'flat world' see Thomas L. Friedman, The World is Flat: The Globalized World in the Twenty-First Century (London: Penguin Books, 2006).

[23] Paul R. Pillar, "Terrorism Goes Global: Extremist Groups Extend Their R each Worldwide," Brookings Institution, 23 February 2009.

traditional-formal-hierarchical of the old. Pyramids have been flattened with multiple leaders wielding authority. Decision making and operations are decentralised, allowing for local initiative and autonomy.[24]

Although network-based structure existed earlier, what is new is the professional way of networking in the globalised world. Most of the present day militant groups prefer operating in small, dispersed and autonomous entities, but linked by advanced communications and "shared principles, interests and goals – at best an overreaching doctrine or ideology – that spans all nodes and to which their members wholeheartedly subscribe."[25] Simon and Benjamin term such arrangement as a combination of "a 'hub and spoke' structure (where nodes communicate with the centre) with a 'wheel' structure (where nodes in the network communicate with each other without reference to the centre)."[26] Overall, the structure "sometimes appear acephalous (headless), and at the other times polycephalous (Hydra-headed)."[27] This phenomenon is called by various names: "leaderless resistance", "phantom cell networks", "network of networks", "lone wolves" and "franchise terrorism".[28] Such structure gives them more flexibility and adaptiveness to the rapidly evolving situations. The network form also increases their resilience as even few of its constituent entities are destroyed, the others carry on.[29]

For training, they tend to utilise more of 'how to do' or 'do it yourself' sources freely available on the Internet and for physical/weapons training take the help of freelance, retired or disbanded

---

[24] Ian Lesser et al, *Countering the New Terrorism* (Santa Monica, CA: Rand, 1999), p. 51.

[25] Ibid.

[26] Steven Simon and Daniel Benjamin, "America and the New Terrorism,"*Survival*, Vol. 42, No. 1, 2000, p. 70.

[27] John Arquilla, David Ronfeldt & Michele Zanini, "Networks, Netwa r, and Information-Age Terrorism", in I. O. Lesser et al. , *Countering the New T errorism* (Santa Monica: RAND , 1999), p. 51.

[28] Raymond Whitaker, "Bin Laden hunt stepped up ," *Canberra Times*, 22 March 2004.

[29] David Tucker, "What's New About the New Terrorism and How Dangerous Is It?" *Terrorism and Political Violence*, Vol. 13, Autumn, 2001, p. 1.

military personnel. They are not only trained just in the military art, but also the "black arts".[30] Amateur groups prefer taking short-term training courses from established terrorist groups. For instance, cadres of Indian Mujahedeen are trained by Lashkar-e-Toiba in Pakistan. It is due to this amorphous nature the modern day VNSAs are difficult to spot and counteract.[31] Their anonymous nature is further reinforced by their disinterestedness to claim credit for their attacks. According to a statistics, only about 30 per cent of all terrorist attacks in 2004 were claimed.[32]

Wide-ranging Motivation:

The rabid motivation of present day VNSAs also lies in "inhuman hatred, all-consuming ill-will and raging fanaticism"[33] in addition to personal vengeance. The new terror groups have "radically different value systems, mechanisms of legitimisation and justification, concepts of morality and Manichean world views".[34] For "the religious terrorist, violence is first and foremost a sacramental act or divine duty executed in direct response to some theological demand or imperative."[35] The struggle is seen as "good against the evil" and therefore large-scale violence is morally justified as necessary for the advancement of their religious cause. They hold themselves accountable to none other than to "their own God" or their representatives.[36] The inevitability of their victory is taken for granted for "God too plans" for them and "would grant victory".[37]

---

[30] Col. Russ Howard, "The New Terrorism," MIT Security Studies Program Seminar, 09 March 2005.

[31] David Tucker, "What's New About the New Terrorism and How Dangerous Is It?"*Terrorism and Political Violence*, Vol. 13, Autumn, 2001, p. 2.

[32] Craig Whitlock, "Terror Probes Find 'the Hands, but Not the Brains'," *Washington Post*, 12 July 2005. Also see Bruce Hoffman, "Why Terrorists Don't Claim Credit," *Terrorism and Political Violence*, Vol. 9, No. 1, Spring 1997, pp. 1-6.

[33] B. S. Raghavan, Fight the War on New Terrorism to the Finish," http://www.rediff.com//news/2008/may/14guest1.htm

[34] Bruce Hoffman, *Inside Terrorism* (New York: Columbia University Press, 2006), p. 88.

[35] Ibid., pp. 88-89.

[36] Bruce Hoffman, "'Holy Terror': The Implications of Terrorism Motivated by a Religious Imperative", *Studies in Conflict and Terrorism*, Vol. 18, No. 4, (1995), p. 273.

[37] Gamat al-Islamiya (Islamic Group), "Statement on US Sentencing of Sheikh Rahman," 19 January 1996.

Suicide attacks are mostly "motivated by the desire for revenge and retaliation" rather than out of deprivation or love for a political cause. Religion, especially, has emerged as a predominant impetus for terrorist attacks.[38] Significantly, most of the Islamist terrorists have deep hatred towards the West in general and the United States in particular. A fatwa issued by the 'World Islamic Front: Jihad Against Jews and Crusaders' on 23 February 1998 pointed out "the ruling to kill the Americans and their allies—civilians and military—is an individual duty of every Muslim who can do it in any country in which it is possible to do it ..."[39] Osama bin Laden made "holy war" between Islam and the Western world as his sole mission and went on to invoke religion to spur terrorist attacks.

Large & Innocent Victims:

Attacks by VNSAs have become bloodier. Accordingly, the choice of victims has been indiscriminate. The aim is no longer to conduct 'propaganda by deed' but to effect maximum destruction[40] as evident in attacks like Oklahoma City Bombing, the Tokyo subway attacks by the Aum Shinrikyo cult, Kobar Towers in Saudi Arabia, 9/11, London train bombings and more recently Mumbai attacks. The aim is to seek the total collapse of their opponents.[41] As some experts aptly put it, "They believe that their violence is divinely justified and that great goals require dramatic means, and the dramatic means is mass bloodshed."[42] This is evident in the increase in the number of

---

[38] Kumar Ramakrishna & Andrew Tan, "The New Terrorism: Diagnosis and Prescriptions" in Andrew Tan & Kumar Ramakrishna (eds.), *The New Terrorism – Anatomy, Trends and Counter-Strategies*, (Singapore: Eastern Universities Press, 2002), pp. 6. According to Nadine Gurr and Benjamin Cole only two out of sixty-four international terrorist organisations in 1980 could be classified as religious. This figure has risen sharply to twenty-five out of fifty-eight by 1995. By 2009, religious-based terrorist groups were predominant. See Nadine Gurr & Benjamin Cole, *The New Face of Terrorism: Threats from Weapons of Mass Destruction*, (London: I.B. Tauris, 2000), pp. 28-29.

[39] Quoted in Yonah Alexander and Michael S. Swetnam, *Usama bin Laden's al Qaida: Profile of a Terrorist Network* (Ardsley: Transnational, 2001), Appendix 1 B.

[40] Walter Lauquer, *No End to War* (New York: Continuum 2003), p. 9.

[41] Dore Gold, *The American Spectator*, March/April 2003.

[42] Karen DeYoung and Michael Dobbs, "The New Terrorism: Global in Scope, it's Based not on Politics but Fervor,"*The Washington Post*, 18 September 2001.

casualties per attack. For instance, 0.17 per cent of international terrorist attacks in 1995-1999 caused 67 per cent of the casualties.[43] They are "freed from ordinary constraints of morality. ... There is less inhibition to kill in quantity and a greater willingness to die in the process."[44] Although use of suicide/suicidal tactics existed before, its use is more predominant now because martyrdom is seen as a way of reaching heaven. The 'suicide terrorist production line'[45] has become easier than ever before.[46]

Urban Terrain Preferred:

In this regard, urban terrain holds significant advantages for VNSAs. It is in urban areas where targets are most varied and abundant: laymen, officials, foreign nationals, corporate heavy weights, government buildings with symbolic/strategic value, bus stands, railway stations, airports, markets, foreign embassies, communication centres etc. By attacking high profile symbolic targets, the terrorists wish to make a point that if a government fails to protect high value targets, it is obvious that it may not be in a position to protect the normal ones. As a result, the credibility of the government of the day is undermined. Since the quality and quantity of terrorists' 'defined enemy' is high in cities, the impact of a destructive act is more widespread. Urban operations for terrorists also often demand less in the way of brute physical strength and endurance than do operations in mountainous or rural terrain.[47] And they do not

---

[43] The US State Department's *Patterns of Global Terrorism* (2002), http://www.state.gov/s/ct/rls/crt/2002/pdf/index.htm

[44] Ibid.

[45] The elements of this 'production line' include the establishment of a social contract, the identification of the 'living martyr' (which accrues great prestige within the community), and – in the culminating phase – the production of the final video. See Jerold M. Post, "Addressing the Causes of T errorism Psy chology," paper presented at the International Summit on Democracy, Terrorism and Security, 8-11 March 2005, Madrid.

[46] Except the L TTE and PKK all other terrorist groups that employ(ed) suicide at tacks are religiously motivated.

[47] Edward L. Glaeser and Jesse M. Shapir o, "Cities and Warfare: The Impact of Terrorism on Urban Form," Harvard Institute of Economic Research, Discussion Paper No. 1942, December 2001.

need sophisticated long-range weapons to inflict desired damage. As is the characteristic of urban areas, population is not only high, but also dense. Unlike in rural areas, inhabitants in cities and towns are more heterogeneous that gives more space for anonymity. It is this posture of anonymity that enables the terrorist fish to swim easily; an excellent place for camouflage. For terrorists, logistical support like arms, medicines, food, and lodging are readily available in an average urban area.[48] Manoeuvrability of terrorists is guaranteed by the presence of public and private transportation facilities that are both dependable and unobtrusive. In urban areas, a terrorist group may find it easier to recruit prospective terrorists in a predictable manner, for it is the city that nurtures dissidence in general. Cities are the nerve centres of a country.[49]

Since terrorism is 'propaganda by the deed' the attention seeking goal of the terrorist is well served in the urban environment where the immediate audience is greatest and where representatives of print and electronic media are readily available and quite eager to report. Such coverage also magnifies the fear-generating capabilities of terrorists. If the general population begins to fear, the objective of a terrorist group may have been achieved. Overall, an urban landscape facilitates terrorists in realising their goals: surprise, maximum damage with minimum risk, hyper media attention and subsequent disappearance.[50]

Their Attacks are More Lethal:

Attacks launched by present day VNSAs are more lethal in character. Accordingly, their choice of weaponry, techniques, and tactics are made to meet the objective of causing mass casualties in a more

---

[48] "Why is Terrorism an Urban Phenomenon?" *Financial Express*, 15 February 2009.

[49] Joshua Woods et al, "Terrorism Risk Perceptions and Proximity to Primary Terrorist Targets: How Close is too Close?" *Human Ecology Review*, Vol. 15, No. 1, 2008, p. 64.

[50] Jo B eall, "Cities, Terrorism and Urban W ars in the 21 st Century," Crisis States Research Centre Working Paper No. 9, February 2009.

lethal manner. They are more "high tech" and their arsenal is not only deadlier, but also more miniature and sophisticated obtained from various sources. Through the general diffusion of scientific skills and dual-use technologies, there is a danger of WMDs falling into the hands of the VNSAs, who wish to use them for mass destruction.[51] For instance, al Qaeda considers as a "religious duty" to acquire WMDs.[52] WMDs are highly destructive, but also difficult to defend and may produce enormous psychological impact because of the sheer fear they inspire. They have no taboo, no morality and see no reason to limit extreme violence that might trigger a backlash. Their "purpose is not to intimidate or persuade but rather simply to destroy."[53] The new cohort of terrorists believes that they have to do something spectacular to receive a grand attention. To them, according to Bruce Hoffman, "both the public and media have become increasingly inured or desensitized to the continuing spiral of terrorist violence. Accordingly, these terrorists feel themselves pushed to undertake ever more dramatic or destructively lethal deeds today in order to achieve the same effect that a less ambitious or bloody action may have had in the past. Indiscriminate lethal attacks against civilians are also motivated to demonstrate that the state is incapable of protecting its citizens."[54] They feel driven by the urge to surpass previous "body counts" and the scale of destruction. Thus, there is an unrelenting upward spiral of violence.

---

[51] For a mor e detailed look at terrorism and WMDs see: Richar d A. Falkenrath, Robert D. Newman, and Bradley A. Thayer, *America's Achilles' heel: nuclear, biological, and chemical terrorism and co vert at tack,* (Cambridge: MIT, 1998); Jessica Stern, "Getting and Using the Weapons" in Russell D. Howard & Reid L. Slayer (eds.) *Terrorism and Counterterrorism – Understanding the New Security Environment* , (Guildford: McGraw-Hill, 2003),

[52] Osama bin Laden's interview to Rahimullah Yusufzai dated 23 December 1998. cited in Ben Venzke and Aimee Ibrahim, *The al Qaeda Threat: An Analytical Guide to al Qaeda's Tactics and Targets* (Alexandria: Tempest Publishers, 2003), p . 53.

[53] David Tucker, "What's New About the New Terrorism and How Dangerous Is It?" *Terrorism and Political Violence* , Vol. 13, Autumn, 2001, p. 3.

[54] Bruce Hoffman, "Terrorism: Trends and Prospects," in Ian Lesser et al, *Countering the New Terrorism* (Santa Monica, CA: R and, 1999), p . 13.

Diverse Support Systems:

VNSAs do not operate in a vacuum. They are often supported, harbored, or tolerated by state actors. Today one can see resources from many countries for VNSAs routed through a single organisation or state. Diverse state sponsorship has, in fact, acted as a "force multiplier" by enhancing planning, intelligence, logistical capabilities, training, finances, and sophistication making VNSAs more akin to elite commando units. Cover of state sovereignty is necessary for them to function and move about effectively, but also for financial support and sanctuary. For instance, Al Qaeda could not have functioned effectively without the help of Afghanistan under Taliban. In the present context, Taliban and Al Qaeda cannot operate without the help of Pakistan.

In addition, support from non-state "amorphous constituencies" has swollen.[55] A new dimension of private sponsorship has also come to the fore. Now individuals like Osama bin Laden run foundations like Al Qaeda to support terrorist projects he considers worthy. At the same time, declining costs for conducting terrorist attacks have increased the confidence of terrorist groups to become less independent of state sponsors. The modern day terrorist groups have also been increasingly relying on their own income generation through illegal sources such as drug trafficking, human smuggling, video piracy and credit card fraud, as well as legal business investments, donations from wealthy individuals, charities and Diaspora.[56] Due to advanced communication and information technology appealing to their supporters and sympathizers, near and far, has become very easy.

---

[55] Mathew J. Morgan, "Origins of New T errorism,"*Parameters*, Spring 2004, p. 37. Also see Jessica Stern, *The Ultimate Terrorists* (Cambridge, Mass.: Harva rd Univ. Press, 1999).

[56] Nimrod Raphaeli, "Financing of Terrorism: Sources, Methods, and Channels", *Terrorism and Political Violence* Vol. 15, No. 4, (2003), pp. 59-82.

Tackling VNSAs

The VNSAs are "**a threat to all states and to all peoples,** which can strike anytime, anywhere."[57] Yet, the world has not fully grappled with the ways to deal with this new form of threat. Presence of violent NSAs has added layers of complexity to traditional conflict management and resolution. Yet another issue is blurred distinction between combatants and non-combatants caused by VNSAs. Any attempts at intervention in such conflicts has been particularly challenging given the fact that international law and norms governing the use of force for intervention or peacekeeping purposes has been primarily written in the context of the nation-state. Presently, there is no single counter-VNSA policy. There are two broad approaches, however as given below:

1. **Realist Approach:** That emphasizes use of force or deterrence to eliminate the VNSAs completely or to pressurize them to adapt to the changing situation. Mechanisms normally used are "hard" options like coercion, control, containment, isolation, division, blackmail and bribery. The problem, however, is NSAs are less deterrable than state actors.[58] In this regard, deterrence can be effectively used against those states that shelter and support VNSAs. Yet another problem with the use of force is some VNSAs tend to demonstrate the change in behavior only as long the force is applied; once the force is off, they get back to their maximalist positions, but now with even more hardline manner. Hence this method is considered as less sustainable.

2. **Institutional/Constructivist Approach:** That seeks to change in interests, policies and norms of VNSAs using "soft"

---

[57] Kofi Anan, " A Global Str ategy for Fighting T errorism," K eynote Address to the Closing Plenary of the I nternational Summi t on Democr acy, Terrorism and S ecurity, 10 Mar ch 2005.

[58] Robert Nurick, "Dealing with Non-State Actor ," 20th I nternational Workshop on 'T oward Global Security: New Str ategies, Technologies, and All iances,' Moscow, 27-30 June 2003.

tactics like persuasion, bargaining, mediation, cooption, negotiation, integration, socialization, naming and shaming and amnesty. This method is considered sustainable because of the underlying assumption that the VNSAs, like state actors, are also concerned about their own legitimacy, image and moral authority.

The above two approaches are not watertight, but generally used in combination. It is important to have a nuanced understanding of the characteristics, strengths and vulnerabilities of VNSAs across their life cycle and also the conflict dynamics to formulate suitable counter-strategy. Such a strategy should not only be comprehensive incorporating political, military, diplomatic and economic aspects, but also consistent and workable. The strategy should be in a position to modify the social, economic and political environment in which VNSAs operate so as to weaken the VNSAs, but also to enable force multipliers towards conflict resolution. Most importantly, the strategy should have consensus of all the concerned actors of the conflict.

Basis for any counter-VNSA policy, at the outset, should be 'zero tolerance': violence as a means of redressing grievances is unacceptable under any circumstances. Addressing the 'root causes' of grievances are vital. Some of the important 'root causes' that require immediate attention include deprivation, inequity, religious intolerance, discrimination, etc. By neutralizing the causes most, if not all, militants can be dissuaded from resorting to violence as a means of achieving their ends. Appropriate methods should be used to prevent and as well to deter VNSAs. Appropriateness is such that "one does not use a tank to catch field mice—a cat will do the job better."[59]

Multi-pronged and multilateral approach and solidarity within the international community is imperative. The strategies should involve

---

[59] Charles Foley (ed.), *The Memoirs of General Grivas* (London: Longmans, 1964), p. 71.

the prevention and elimination of sources of violence wherever they are rooted, effective mechanisms of sanctions, trans-national cooperation of all law enforcement authorities. Despite 12 international treaties relating to terrorism, a comprehensive convention covering all aspects of counterterrorism is missing. Such a convention should be powerful enough to deter states from supporting VNSAs. The multilateralism should not prevent states from having bilateral arrangements aimed at enhancing intelligence ties between the security agencies of their countries, mutual sharing of database and experience on counterterrorism and joint training/exercise of their forces.

At the same time, the fight must be compatible with fundamental freedoms and human rights. The argument is, if we compromise on 'core values'[60] in our response, we are handing a victory to the VNSAs. In other words, any counter-VNSA strategy's disregard for human rights keeps alive the underlying tension, hatred and mistrust of government among precisely those parts of the population where VNSAs are most likely to find recruits. A vicious circle should not start all over again.

Conclusion

Very few states today can claim a monopoly of force within their respective territorial boundaries. Pervasive challenge to the state sovereignty comes from VNSAs, who pose "tier-one" security threat. Amorphous nature of present day organizational structure of terrorist groups is deliberate to not only to thwart any easy identification but also to facilitate escape of the terrorists. The 'new terrorism' is more lethal claiming more casualties than ever before. Religion and revenge factors constitute major ingredients of motivation to the new cohort

---

[60] The United Nations identifies these 'core values' as the rule of law; the protection of civilians; mutual respect between people of different faiths and cultures; and peaceful resolution of conflict.

of terrorists. They are high-tech, professional and leave fewer footprints.[61] The present day VNSAs are difficult to penetrate. The funding for them has become diverse and, at the same time, opaque. Therefore, it is difficult to identify and fully block the funding sources. Since the target of the new form of terrorism has become more urban oriented, it gives an added advantage to terrorists to prevent any kind of indiscriminate counter-terrorist operation by the state that could maximise collateral damage. For the same reason, use of aerial bombardments against the terrorists becomes difficult. What is required is a comprehensive approach and support of the international community to tackle VNSAs.

---

[61] Raymond Whitaker and Paul Lashmar, "Franchise terrorism: 'Trying to hit al-Qa'ida is like trying to hit jel ly'," *The Independent*, 10 July 2005.

Non-State Actors in South Asia: The Actors and Challenges

Maj Gen G D Bakshi SM, VSM (Retd)

Historical Perspective. The Af-Pak region in South Asia today is the global hub of Jihadi terrorism. Thousands of its Madrassas form a Jihad factory and primary incitory network for terrorist strikes across the globe. This Jihad has had its major spill over into J&K in the form of the Proxy War that lasted for two decades. Finding troop density too high in J&K, the ISI in 2007-08 spread the Jihad to Indian cities via the Indian Mujahideen (IM) using localised Tanzeems with local narratives.

Blowback Effect. In the biggest blowback in the history of covert operations, the Afghan Jihad ended up with 9/11 and caused a tectonic paradigm shift. It has now badly singed Pakistan and could lead to a major faultline crack emerging along the Indus River. Pakistan has now adopted the narrative of victimhood. Its travails however are a clear outcome of the conscious choices it made and the deliberate chaos it has engineered in the region. The non-state actors now targeting Pakistan are its specific creation designed to destabilize India and Afghanistan. The ISI is clearly involved in all Jihadi attacks on Indian soil. The zero sum game of the Pak Military-ISI Complex in Islamabad is at the root of the region's problems. The Bleeding Hearts Brigade's desire for peace with Pakistan at *any cost* must take cognizance of this harsh reality.

Left Wing Extremism (LWE). Maoist violence virtually overthrew the state in Nepal. It had graduated to regular and large scale military operations against the Royal Nepal Army (RNA). The effort to integrate the Maoists into the democratic mainstream is seriously floundering. It has provided the Chinese with a major ideological bridgehead for the destabilisation of South Asia. Our former support to the Maoists amounts to a self goal that could have serious long-term repercussions. In India, LWE has now become the most serious threat to national security. The People's Guerilla Army is now graduating to large-scale mobile operations. The heavy casualties suffered by the CRPF/Police clearly indicate that it is fast graduating beyond the capability levels of the Police/PMF and may need a military response. Howsoever much we may want to avoid it, the country may soon be left with no other option.

What do the events in the Af-Pak region and Maoist violence have in common?

Non-State Actors: Crafting a South Asian Perspective. Though apparently unrelated, there is a core commonality in the threats to security posed by the Non-State Actors in South Asia. The primary threat stems from the failure of the South Asian states to integrate their tribal populations into the national mainstream. Thus the violence in NWFP, Swat, and FATA in Pakistan; Maoist violence in Nepal and in the Red corridor in India, is the manifestation of the failure of states to integrate their long marginalized tribal societies. In the Af-Pak region, the problem has been severely compounded by the induction of Jihad ideology and the massive infusion of small arms/explosives into these highly militarized tribal societies. Pakistan has launched an all out military offensive using firepower/airpower to 'mass effects' to subdue the tribes in South Waziristan and Swat. So far, it has achieved temporary neutralization. It remains to be seen how effective this strategy would be in the long term. If it fails, Pakistan could well break up along the ethnic faultline of the Indus river.

Tribe-Ideology Combinations in South Asia

AF-PAK

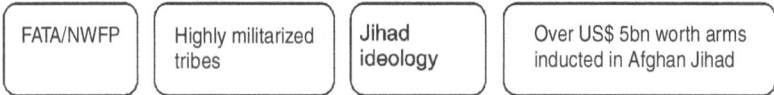

| FATA/NWFP | Highly militarized tribes | Jihad ideology | Over US$ 5bn worth arms inducted in Afghan Jihad |

NEPAL

| Magar Gurung Tribes | Highly militarized tribes | Maoist Ideology | Leadership by Urban Intellectuals |

INDIA

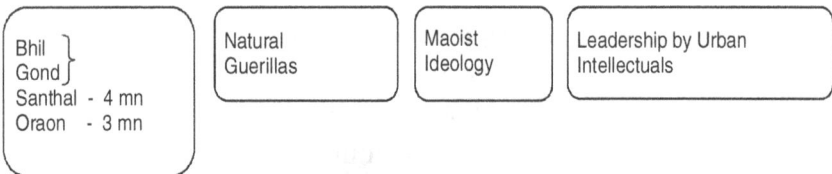

| Bhil ⎱ Gond ⎰ Santhal - 4 mn Oraon - 3 mn | Natural Guerillas | Maoist Ideology | Leadership by Urban Intellectuals |

Historical Legacy Conflicts. India was politically united only thrice in its long history, by the Mauryan Empire, Mughal Empire and the British Empire. All three were based on revenue from taxation on agricultural surplus. As such, they did not find it cost-effective to penetrate tribal lands in dense forests/barren hills, as these did not yield any taxable revenue surplus (being subsistence economies). All these empires therefore consciously left the tribes alone. They did not find it worthwhile to carry out administrative/infrastructural penetration in these regions. The neglect after independence has been callous. Today, the integration of these marginalized tribal regions will involve serious military pacification and major administrative/ infrastructural penetration efforts. In India, this simply cannot be avoided as 85% of India's mineral resources of Coal, Iron, Aluminum and Uranium are in these regions.

Jihad Ideology and Mindset. Communist ideology and mindset is historically well understood. However Jihad ideology and Non-State Actors/Organisations it spawned in South Asia are a new phenomenon that needs to be studied in depth. An understanding of the Jihadi organisational set up entails first and foremost an understanding of this ideological outlook. Religion is as much an ideology as is Marxism or any other political ideology. In fact the CIA used religion in Afghanistan to defeat the ideology of Marxism. In the bargain, it created a Frankenstein ideology that has now targeted the USA and its values.

Ideological Threat

Roots of Rage. What are the roots of Islamic rage? Why is the Muslim world so angry? It stems primarily from the loss of empire. It must be remembered that in its heydays, the Mughal Empire was generating 25% of the World's GDP. Then came its failure to industrialise and this in turn led to humiliation at the hands of the Western colonial powers. This led to loss of empire and subjugation.

ROOTS OF RAGE

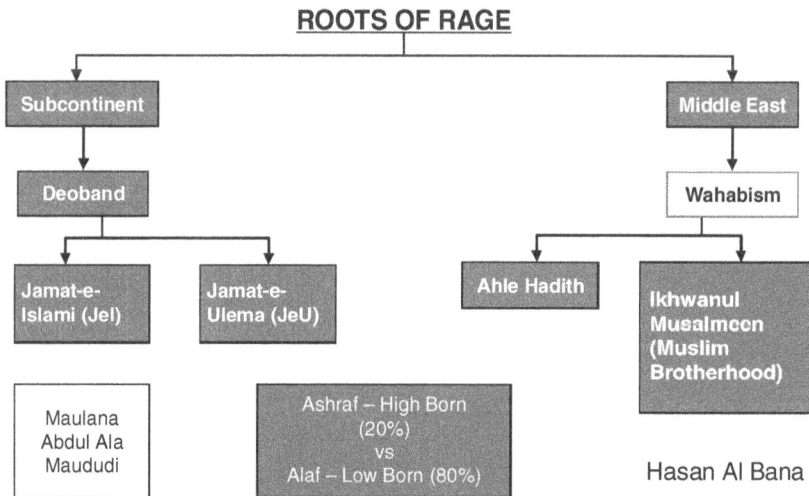

Concept of State Formation: Pakistan

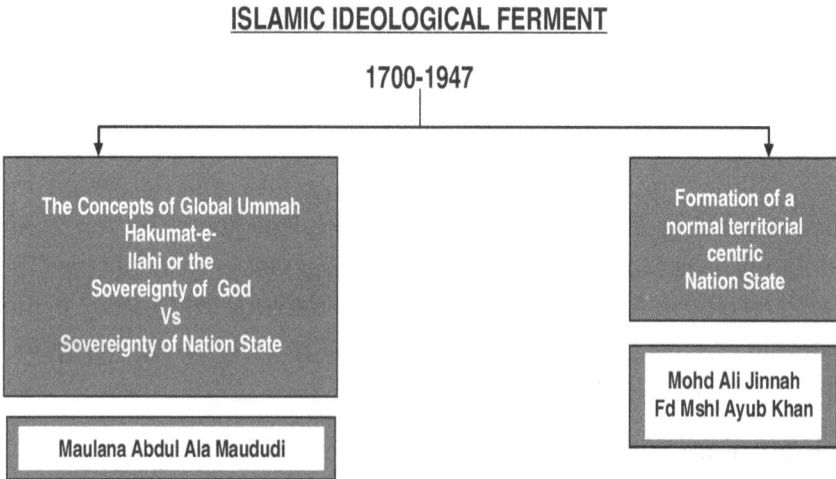

ISLAMIC IDEOLOGICAL FERMENT

1700-1947

The Concepts of Global Ummah Hakumat-e-Ilahi or the Sovereignty of God Vs Sovereignty of Nation State	Formation of a normal territorial centric Nation State
Maulana Abdul Ala Maududi	Mohd Ali Jinnah Fd Mshl Ayub Khan

Al Jihad e Islam. The foremost ideologues of Jihad were Hasan Al Bana of the Ikhwanul Musalmeen (Islamic Brotherhood) and Abdul Ala Maududi – the founder of Jamait e Islami Pakistan. Maududi's book Al Jehad-e-Islam became Gen Zia ul Haq's Bible. He used to gift it at various functions. Concept of Hakumat-e-Ilahi or the sovereignty of God as opposed to the sovereignty of the nation state. State sovereignty was blasphemous. It was 'Fiqh'. Maududi had opposed the idea of Pakistan as a normal territorial centric nation state. The Ummah, he felt was global and could not be confined within national boundaries. Theologically, this argument is seriously flawed. The Lord of the Quran is the lord of the entire 'Kainat' and not just the Lord of 'Musalmeen'. Maududi was greatly impressed by the fanaticism of Fascist/Nazi/Communist cadres. He postulated the concept of asymmetry of will between a minority of fanatics and a moderate majority. He believed in the coercive theory of social change in society. He often cited examples of Nazis and Communists, whose small dedicated groups were able to exercise total control over the whole society. Fascist and undemocratic in outlook, the fundamentalists relied upon the messianic personality of their leaders. Fanatic modules led by Amirs would dominate entire populations into meek submission. Coercive minority of zealots is the very antithesis of democracy and representative form of government.

Afghan Jihad. The Afghan Jihad was an epochal event in recent history.

"The Afghan Jihad was the first successful resistance to a foreign power, which was not based on either nationalist or socialist principles but instead on Islamic principles. It was waged as a Jihad and gave a tremendous boost to Islamic self-confidence and power. Its impact on the Islamic World was in effect, comparable to the impact which the Japanese defeat of the Russians in 1905 had on the Oriental World."

Samuel P. Huntington
The Clash of Civilizations and the Remaking of World Order

"The war left behind an uneasy coalition of Islamic organizations intent on promoting Islam against all non-Muslim forces. It also left a legacy of expert and experienced fighters, camps, training grounds and logistic facilities, elaborate trans-Islam networks of personal and organizational relationships and a substantial amount of military equipment. Most important, it gave a heady sense of power and self-confidence over what had been achieved and a driving desire to move on to other Victories."

Samuel P. Huntington
The Clash of Civilizations and the Remaking of World Order

Growth of Madrassas in Pakistan. There has been an explosive growth of Madrassas in Pakistan. From just 245 at the time of independence, this shot up to 11,882 by 2005. If the number of unregistered Madrassas is included, this adds up to over 45,000. The growth is shown in graphic form below:

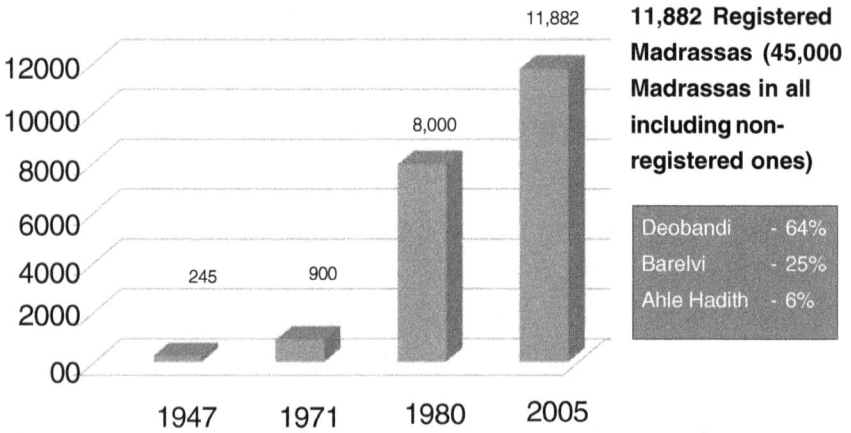

Chart data: 1947: 245, 1971: 900, 1980: 8,000, 2005: 11,882

11,882 Registered Madrassas (45,000 Madrassas in all including non-registered ones)

Deobandi   - 64%
Barelvi   - 25%
Ahle Hadith - 6%

International Islamic Front. In the starting of August 1996, Osama Bin Laden (OBL) issued a series of Fatwas against the USA. In his Fatwas issued in 1996, 1998 and 1999, he incited the Muslims to declare Jihad against the USA. In 1998, the International Islamic Front was created by OBL much on the lines, on which the International Communist Front had operated in the heydays of Communism. It emphasized that all Islamic people were part of one global Ummah. The new concept sought to weave together in one mosaic, all the diverse struggles of Muslims in different parts of the world against one easily identified enemy – the Westernized world led by the USA and its values. OBL infused a new vision and a sense of mission, aimed at establishing the Islamic caliphate. A coalition was formed of Extremist Islamic Organizations, including the Al Qaeda, Taliban, Lashkar-e-Toiba, Jaish-e-Muhammad, HuJI, HuM, Muslim Brotherhood (Egypt), Abu Sayyaf Group (Philippines), Free Acheh Movement (Indonesia), IMET (Xinjiang) etc. In the 9/11 terrorist attacks, aviation fuel laden civil airliners were used as human guided cruise missiles to strike highly symbolic targets in continental US. It was a local tactical action with huge strategic impact. Post 9/11, the American offensive against the Taliban/Al Qaeda in

Afghanistan has severely disrupted the cohesion of this organisation. However, it has become diffused and spread out. Autonomous franchisees have arisen all over the globe and act independently without any central directions. Pakistani Punjab based LeT and JeM are fast becoming global organisations. The ISI is the chief patron of the Taliban. It directly funds, arms and trains Hekmatyar's Lashkar-e-Ishar and the Jalaluddin Haqqani group. Former ISI operatives of the afghan Jihad have been entrusted with the task of liasing with the Taliban.

Use of Ideology

"Unfortunately during the process of the tactical use of ideology to further short term agendas and narrow political and personal objectives, the very character and chemistry of Pakistani state was changed forever. Today, Pakistan is at great risk of becoming a theocracy than it ever was before."

Hussain Haqqani
Pakistan: Between Mosque and Military

"Zia ul Haq's use of ideology subverted the very character and nature of Pakistani nation state. From a nation state, he transformed it into an ideological bridgehead for exporting Jihadi causes all over the world."

Vali Nasr
Malaysian Islamic Scholar

Growth of Jihadi Organisations in Pakistan

The following charts trace the growth of Jihadi organisations in Pakistan. The Deobandi group of organisations spawned the Hizbul Mujahideen, Al Badr, Harkat ul Ansar (which later became the Jaish-e-Muhammad) as also the Sipah-e-Saheba (Pakistan).

The Wahabi group of organisations has spawned the dangerous Lashkar-e-Toiba (which is now becoming a group with global reach). It has also spawned the Tehreek-e-Nifaz-e-Shariyat-e-Mohammad (TNSM) and the students organisation called Tehreek-e-Tulba.

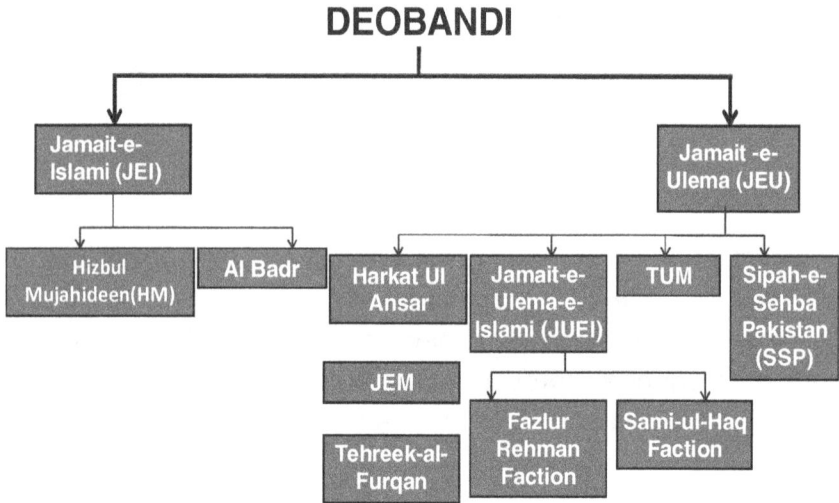

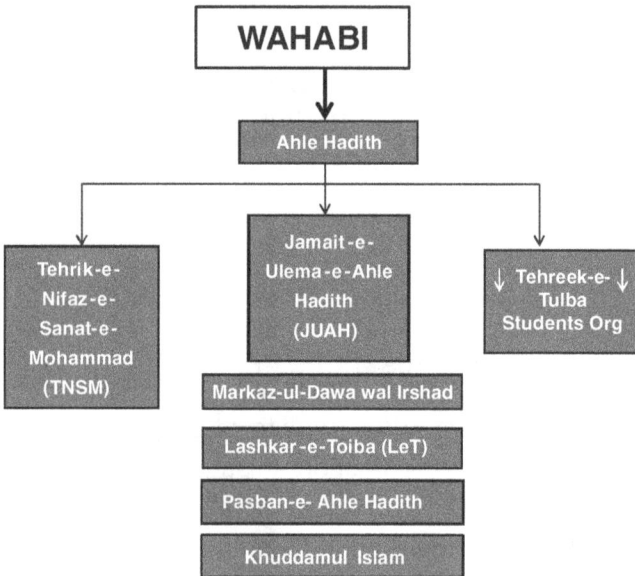

DEOBANDI

```
                        DEOBANDI
                            |
        ┌───────────────────┴───────────────────┐
        ▼                                        ▼
 Jamait-e-                                  Jamait-e-
 Islami (JEI)                               Ulema (JEU)
        |                                        |
   ┌────┴────┐                    ┌──────┬───────┴──────┐
   ▼         ▼                    ▼      ▼        ▼      ▼
 Hizbul    Al Badr         Harkat Ul  Jamait-e-   TUM   Sipah-e-
Mujahideen(HM)             Ansar      Ulema-e-           Sehba
                                      Islami (JUEI)      Pakistan
                                                         (SSP)
              JEM                         ┌────────┴────────┐
                                          ▼                 ▼
          Tehreek-al-                  Fazlur          Sami-ul-Haq
          Furqan                       Rehman          Faction
                                       Faction
```

WAHABI

```
                    WAHABI
                       |
                       ▼
                   Ahle Hadith
                       |
        ┌──────────────┼──────────────┐
        ▼              ▼               ▼
 Tehrik-e-        Jamait-e-       ↓ Tehreek-e- ↓
 Nifaz-e-         Ulema-e-Ahle      Tulba
 Sanat-e-         Hadith            Students Org
 Mohammad         (JUAH)
 (TNSM)
              Markaz-ul-Dawa wal Irshad

              Lashkar-e-Toiba (LeT)

              Pasban-e- Ahle Hadith

              Khuddamul Islam
```

Doctrinal Debate. Ijtihad (independent reasoning), Ijma (consensus of the community) and Hadith (eyewitness reports of the customary practices of the Prophet) are the three pillars of Islam. The first two made Islam a very democratic and liberal faith. However, internecine conflict during the period of the decline of Caliphate led to a decline of legitimacy. This shifted the emphasis heavily away from the Ijma and Ijtihad to the Hadith and to doctrinaire rigidity and intolerance of dissent or debate. This is shown diagrammatically on the next page:-

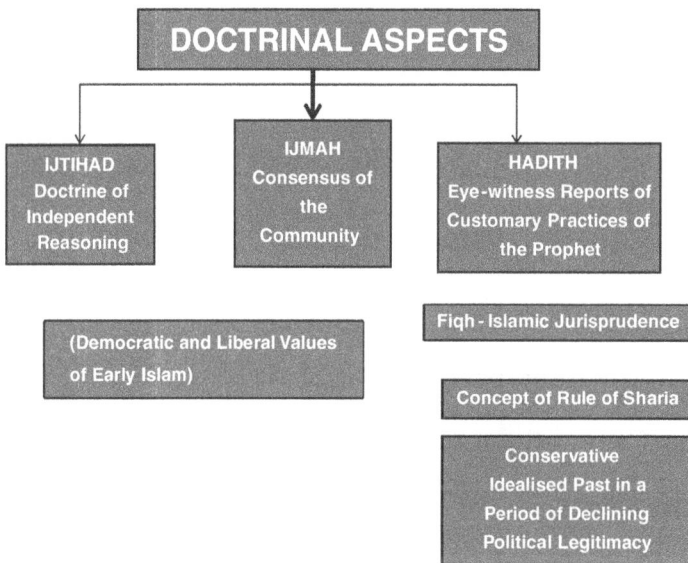

DOCTRINAL ASPECTS

IJTIHAD Doctrine of Independent Reasoning	IJMAH Consensus of the Community	HADITH Eye-witness Reports of Customary Practices of the Prophet

(Democratic and Liberal Values of Early Islam)

Fiqh - Islamic Jurisprudence

Concept of Rule of Sharia

Conservative Idealised Past in a Period of Declining Political Legitimacy

Operational Profile: J&K. The Proxy War in J&K can be studied under three phases:-

(a) **Azadi Phase.** JKLF. (1989-1995). The local JKLF was decimated by 1994-95.

(b) **Jihad Phase.** The ISI then inducted the Jihadi Tanzeems HM, HUM, HUJI, (1996-2006). Later LET & JEM.

    I.   It tried to widen the Arc of Terrorism to south of the Pirpanjals.

    II. **Effect of LC Fence.** The LC Fence was a major game changer. It was a physical obstacle and electronic wall of sensors. It seriously curtailed infiltration of men and arms and ammunition. The choking of arms and ammunition supply was a key component of the defeat mechanism. By 2007, the back of the Terrorist Tanzeems was broken. The overall annual strength of terrorists in J&K was cut down from 3,500 to just around 600.

(c) **Intifada Phase.** The ISI now changed tactics and tried to switch it to a Palestenian style Intifada based on communal mobilisation. It took the form of rioting and arson. Amarnath agitation was its trailor. This assumed serious proportions in 2010 in Kashmir with:

    I.   Mass based Agitations

    II. Communal based mobilisation

    III. Renewed surge of infiltration (Apr 2009)

Local Tanzeems

The new ISI phase of deniability led to greater dependence on local Tanzeems with localized narratives (like Indian Mujahideen (IM)). Smaller logistical foot prints were ensured by avoiding use of RDX, PE or heavy caliber weapons. Locally available chemicals like Ammonium Nitrate, Hydrogen Peroxide, Neogel, Slurry/ industrial explosives- Gelatin/ Dynamite were used. Though less powerful, when used on large scale, these generated mass casualties and panic. There was a minimal electronic signature and a greater need for humint.

Seven camps held in 2007/08 as under :-

(i)   In Apr 07, three camps were held at Castle Rock near Hubli.

(ii) In Aug 07, one camp was held at Dharwad District near Karnataka.

(iii) In Nov 07, a camp was held at Charol near Indore.

(iv) In Dec 07, a camp was held at Nagaman jungles in Kerala.

(v) In Jan 08, a camp was held in Pawagarh jungles near Vadodra.

Major Bomb Blasts

- Mumbai 11 July 07 : 7 blasts in local trains. 200 killed. 700 wounded.

- Hyderabad 26 Aug 07 : 2 blasts. 42 killed. 100 wounded.

- Rampur 01 Jan 08 : Attack on CRPF. 8 killed.

- Jaipur 14 May 08 : 8 blasts. 80 killed. 150 wounded.

- Bangalore 25 Jul 08 : 8 blasts. 1 killed.

- Ahmedabad 26 July 08 : 17 blasts. 53 killed.

- New Delhi 13 Sept 08 : 5 blasts. 26 killed. 90 wounded.

- Guwahati 30 Oct 08 : 9 blasts. 84 killed. 300 wounded.

- Mumbai 26-29 Nov 08 : Small arms attack via the sea. 174 killed. 300 wounded.

Mumbai. Most of the IM modules were rapidly busted by Indian Police. Since Local Tanzeems were relatively easier to penetrate, ISI turned to LeT. Finding most of the land border fenced, the LeT attacked via the sea route. LET had been rehearsing this attack for months. As a switch of tactics, the LeT, instead of using explosives (where only after effects can be recorded by media), resorted to fire arms based attacks and hostage situations to grab eyeballs for three days. The terrorists attacked iconic targets (five star hotels) with high foreign tourists presence to gain international media coverage. This led to a major outrage in the country.

Attack Profiles. Atatck profiles of the future could include:-

    (i)   RDX/TNT based powerful explosive attacks.

    (ii) IM style low intensity explosions in tandem. Multiple strikes to create confusion and multiply media impact

    (iii) Fire arms based attacks on iconic targets / dense population targets:-

        a.   Parliament/Govt buildings.

        b.   Five star hotels.

        c.   Airports, railway stations, metro terminals,shopping malls, bazaars and crowded markets.

        d.   Election rallies and political leaders.

SUPPORTING MECHANISMS AND CATALYSTS FOR NON STATE ACTORS (NSAs) IN SOUTH ASIA

Maj Gen YK Gera (Retd)

Introduction

India has been involved with insurgency since the mid-1950s. A nexus of terrorist and insurgent organizations which operate in the state of Jammu and Kashmir, the North Eastern states and the hinterland of Madhya Pradesh, Chhatisgarh, Maharashtra, Bihar, Jharkhand, Orissa, and Andhra Pradesh appears to be emerging. For the last 63 years or so, India and Pakistan have been neighbours but never friends. One of the annual reports of the Ministry of Home Affairs mentions: *Pakistan has consistently used terrorism and covert actions as an instrument of State policy against India. It has recruited, trained, financed, armed and infiltrated terrorists in India and has provided sanctuaries to anti-Indian elements.*

Insurgency and Terrorism

Insurgency and terrorism have a common aim but the tactics adopted are different. Insurgency relies wholly on the support of the people, and to an extent terrorism also does so, but when this is not forthcoming, the people are terrorized to support. Both are instances of the weak fighting the strong. Massacre of innocents including women and children, kidnappings, hijackings, and taking hostages are practiced by terrorists but not by insurgents.

Types of Terrorism

Secessionist Terrorism. NSAs resort to secessionist terrorism to obtain independence of a certain area from the State. Example – India faces a vicious mix of insurgency, terrorism and proxy war in Jammu and Kashmir.

Revolutionary Terrorism. It may be resorted to by the NSAs to bring about an ideological and economic revolution. Sovereignty of State is questioned but not its integrity. Example – PRC had a revolution led by Mao-tse-Tung.

Jehadi terrorism. It is based on religious fanaticism and hatred for other religions. Is symbolic of struggle between multiculturalism and mono-cultural extremism expressed through terrorist violence. Pakistan has emerged as the epicentre of international terrorism. Taliban in Pakistan and in Afghanistan have emerged as lead elements of Islamic *jehad*. The salient features of their philosophy are – they consider themselves superior to unbelievers; have nostalgia about a glorious past (the *Caliphat*); have contempt for women; glorification of violence; total rejection of democracy and right of individual dissent.

SECURITY SITUATION IN SOUTH ASIA

Growth of Islamic Terrorism

The Soviet troops had occupied Afghanistan. To push them out, Islamic zealots were brought to Pakistan and Afghanistan, forging a unity among them. The Soviet Union had to retreat. It made Islamists aware of the potential of *Jehad* and force multiplication effect of networking. The *Taliban* seized power in Afghanistan. With military backing from Pakistan, they converted Afghanistan into a breeding ground for Islamic terrorists. It became home of Al Qaeda. In South

Asia, in Afghanistan, Pakistan and Bangladesh this virus multiplied prolifically. In India it struck lethally.

Pakistan

The Pakistan Government, right from their founding has supported and encouraged *jihadi* groups, creating an atmosphere that has allowed them to flourish. However; the 11 September 2001 incident changed the global perception of the threat. Pakistan could not support the Taliban and Al Qaeda as before. It took a tactical half summersault and decided to cooperate with the West to the extent it was necessary to protect Pakistan's strategic interests. Pakistan made queer deals and counter deals with both sides. The ISI of Pakistan had used rival Islamic groups selectively, but is now finding it difficult to live with its contradictions.

There are three broad categories of terrorist groups in Pakistan. The first category targets the West; the second perpetuates domestic violence and the third targets India. Pakistan is finding it difficult to cope with the dichotomy created by its unprincipled policy. The terrorist groups operating in India continue to receive state patronage. The training camps and other infrastructure have not been rolled back, though greater discretion is exercised. The problem of terrorism across border is set to continue.

Afghanistan

The Taliban - Al Qaeda combine appear to have regrouped especially in provinces dominated by *Pashtuns* along the Pakistan –Afghan border. Pakistan has evidently allowed the combine; use of its territory to launch attacks across the border. Despite selective military operations in the Federally Administered Tribal Areas (FATA) and the North West Frontier Province (NWFP), there is no indication to suggest that Pakistan has any intension of cutting the Taliban's lifeline on its soil. It shares strategic goals with the Taliban in this theatre. The US led counterterrorism operations continue in Afghanistan.

Bangladesh

After the 11 September 2001 incident, Pakistan and Afghanistan came under pressure by the international community. A number of terrorists, reportedly with support of the ISI of Pakistan found Bangladesh a safe haven. Using Islamic card, most local groups are working on the franchise of Pakistan-Afghanistan terrorist outfits including Al Qaeda. The collective strength of Islamic terrorist groups is estimated to be in thousands. India is the principal target.

India has been trying to get the issue of militancy from across the Bangladesh borders addressed. The Awami League government appears to be moving cautiously against the *Jehadi* groups. If the war on terror in Pakistan and Afghanistan does not come to a positive conclusion, the situation can also deteriorate in Bangladesh. India's security concerns are unlikely to be addressed fully.

The illegal migration from Bangladesh has also turned out to be a major security threat. The illegal migrants often act as sleeper cells for terror organizations like HUJI. Acting against illegal migration is not going to be easy for any government.

Maldives

The Maldives, with its Muslim majority and a strategic location, is a target for expansion of *jehadi* activities in the Indian Ocean region. In September 2007 there was a bomb explosion at Male's Sultan Park and 12 foreign tourists were injured. Roots of the bomb blast were traced to Pakistan[1]. Reports indicate that the LeT is seeking bases in uninhabited islands in this region from where weapons and explosives could be smuggled into the coastal states of India.

Nepal, Bhutan and Sri Lanka

In Nepal Maoist insurgency had been going on since 1996. In April 2006, Maoists decided to contest elections after laying down arms.

---

[1] Maj Gen (Retd) Afsir Karim, ' The Persistent Menace', *AAKROSH, (New Delhi)* p9, January 2010, Volume 13 Number 46.

They have joined the main stream. Bhutan has good friendly relations with India. Illegal presence of militant camps using Bhutan as the base came to light. On 15 December 2003, the Royal Bhutan Army launched military operations and flushed out the militants. In Sri Lanka, LTTE had been conducting insurgency for more than three decades. The Sri Lankan Forces succeeded in wiping out the LTTE in May 2009.

India

India has witnessed full impact of militant Islam through Pakistan, ranging from infiltrations to aerial high-jacking to series of bomb blasts in the cities. The proxy war in Jammu and Kashmir continues with infiltration of terrorists from Pakistan. Indian embassy in Kabul was attacked. A commando assault took place in Mumbai on 26 November 2008, the after effects of which are still continuing. The violence has all along been carefully calibrated by the ISI of Pakistan to ensure continuance of terrorism. At the same time, it has ensured that the terrorist activities do not cross the threshold of India's tolerance without allowing it to fall below a point from which it could be difficult to revive. In short we have to live with terrorism for more time and need to keep abreast with techniques for countering it.

The rise of Left Wing Extremism (LWE) is a dangerous development. It is a secessionist movement. Their demands centering around *"jal, jungle and jamin"* strike a populist chord. They are able to drum up support in media also. It has built up a robust military structure. India is lagging behind tremendously as far as land reforms are concerned. Despite land ceiling laws, only 1.25 per cent of land has been redistributed. Over 160 districts are affected by Maoist violence. Planned attacks, ambushes and use of IED blasts are made by them. The security forces are handicapped due to poor government machinery in the affected areas, poor governance, and thick forests.

India has two major areas of concern- Islamic *jehadi* terrorism fanned and supported by Pakistan and the LWE.

SUPPORTING MECHANISMS

The Cause

Terrorist groups like Al-Qaeda and LeT seek to establish a universal Islamic *Caliphate* with emphasis on realizing this dream through gradual recovery of lands that were once under Muslim rule. This is considered a holy cause by Muslims and has tremendous appeal.

Change in Security Environment

Security environment has changed radically. Economic security and energy security have attained higher priority. Asymmetric warfare rather than conventional, is the order of the day globally. An adversary will seek to wage asymmetric warfare and cripple the economic and energy infrastructure by means of lethal weapons and munitions with far less risk than engaging military targets.

Force Multiplication Effect of Networking

Realisation of Potential. The Soviet troops had occupied Afghanistan. To push them out, Islamic zealots were brought from all parts of the Islamic world to Pakistan and Afghanistan. The Soviet Union had to retreat. It made Islamists aware of the potential of *jehad* and force multiplication effect of networking. The development and proliferation of Internet has enabled rise of loose, decentralized networks of international terrorists, guerrilla insurgents, groups smuggling narcotics, and tribal gangs working towards a common goal.

Analysis of 11 September 2001 Terrorist Strikes. Al Qaeda used networks for conduct of 11 September 2001 strikes in New York and Washington D C. The operation was planned in Germany, funded by countries in West Asia, approved in Afghanistan and executed in the USA. In the long run "effectiveness" matters in war. Thus it is important to have modern network systems and exploit them with ingenuity to attain organizational goals. Al Qaeda made extensive use of the existing international infrastructure for launch of its mission as under:-

(a) Used Internet for recruitment of terrorists.

(b) For training, simulators and existing aviation schools in the USA were used.

(c) For coordination, cell phones using international telecommunication systems.

Availability of Mobile Cell Phones. Terrorists buy pre-activated SIMs of foreign service providers[2] through some agents based say in New Delhi. Calls from such mobiles are reflected on the Indian network as calls from a foreign country, where the SIM issuing company is actually based and registered, while the caller might be calling from next door. Government guidelines lay down that country specific SIMs sold in India should work only when they are used in that country. For flouting of orders and improper verification, the service providers should be jailed. In practice it has not been happening.

Radicalisation of Locals

Radical Islamic activity across India has seen a rapid increase. There are sleeper cells of LeT, JeM, HUJI and others. During the last couple of years more than 1,000 modules and cells have been destroyed. However, many hundreds still exist. Home grown Islamic insurgency SIMI is a major promoter of violence and remains wedded to the reinstatement of the *Caliphate.*

Political Support to NSAs in India

India is a multi-ethnic society and a multi-party democracy. Parties have strategies for garnering and protecting their vote banks. The RJD and SP are chary of imposing a ban on SIMI. The PDP in J&K

[2.] Times of India, (New Delhi) p1, 27 March 2010.

is known to be supporting the militants. Mr AB Bardan of CPI said at a meeting of Left parties- *Left should fight against government attempts to club our Naxalites' brothers with extremists. Left's goals and Naxalites' are same, they have adopted a different approach. We must lend them support and condemn government's attempt to club them with extremists.*

Control over Explosives and Weapons

In India there are 21,000 licensed manufacturers of explosives. A lot of pilferage is reported from them. In two years period, there was reported loss of 20,200 kgs of industrial explosives and 86,899 detonators. Just two companies, Rajasthan Explosives and Chemicals Limited and Andhra Pradesh Explosives Limited produce 60 million detonators per year. At this rate, it can be imagined as to how much explosives and detonators are being produced by 21,000 licensed companies. Why do we need so many licensed companies? A review is necessary. The Fertilizer Ministry is reluctant to impose instructions for checks of sale of Ammonium Nitrate based fertilizers (used as explosives), saying that it would affect the profitability of fertilizer companies. Such arguments should be rejected because it is a matter of life and death for the personnel of the security forces; has adverse effect on their morale and is not in the interest of national security.

Strict control is required on holding of private weapons. Issue of new licenses for arms must be stopped. Weapons in the environment must be taken away from all people except the security forces

Drug Trafficking and Money Laundering

Annual profits generated by the narcotics industries are estimated at several billion US dollars. The major production and trafficking complexes representing the world's most successful illegal enterprises are in the Latin Americas, the Golden Crescent (Afghanistan, Iran and Pakistan) and the Golden Triangle (Cambodia,

Laos, Thailand and Vietnam). The drug trade is backed by armed gangs to give protection to distributors to enforce verbal transactions, subdue and intimidate law enforcement agencies and terrorize politicians and informers. The disturbed conditions in the Northwest and North East States of India which are geographically close to major narcotics areas- the Golden Crescent and the Golden Triangle are ominous. Some of the problems endemic in those areas are possibly supported by revenues derived from the drug trade.

Counterfeit Currency

Counterfeit currency is used to finance terrorists. As per reports, there are 6,000 crore pieces of currency notes valued at 1,69,000 crores in circulation in India. Many insurgent groups are known to be involved in large scale extortion, drug trafficking, running illegal business and so on. It has been learnt that the ISI of Pakistan has set up printing facilities for printing counterfeit Indian currency in Quetta and in Bangkok by Aftab Bakti a known aide of ISI protected Dawood Ibrahim.

Weak Judicial System

The political parties and state administration must effectively occupy the political, administrative and judicial space in J&K, North East and Maoist affected areas. Such spaces cannot be left as a void to be filled in by militants. It is the duty of the State to recover taxes as per national legislations and not allow anyone else to indulge in tax collection and extortion. Judicial sentences must be in accordance with national norms. A judiciary which is aligned to the militants' cause or is too scared, cannot function in an acceptable manner, hence there is a need to bring in more outsiders and bring in tougher legislation, since that is the need of the hour to fight the anti-national elements.

Role of Media

Media thrives on sensationalism. It acts as oxygen for terrorists. During acts of terrorism, terrorists have the initiative and media is eager to put across at the earliest whatever they can grab. Terrorists seem to hog the media coverage. Media needs to be made more accountable. Military's media handling is only reactive in most cases.

Proxy War by Pakistan

Deniable Instrument of State Apparatus. India is convinced that LeT is sponsored by the Pakistan Government. The connections between the LeT and the ISI of Pakistan are well known, as are LeT's various camps and offices in Pakistan. India considers LeT an extension of Pakistan state apparatus, albeit with some degree of deniability. Indian officials believe that terrorism is official Pakistani policy. India is likely to remain a target of Pakistan based terrorism till such time as Pakistan is compelled to dismantle the terrorist infrastructure comprehensively. With the arrest of two suspected LeT terrorists- David Headley and his accomplice Tahawwur Rana, in the US, involved in supporting 26 November 2008 terrorist attacks in Mumbai, it has become obvious that the LeT has increased its reach considerably. The Headley- Rana network was unraveled by the FBI. As per media report, Headley has named five serving Pakistan Army officers- Colonel Shah, Majors Samir Ali, Iqbal and two more; who are among the leaders of Karachi Project terrorist operation being planned to be launched in India by the LeT. The revelation by Headley and uncovering of money laundered in Italy to support the Mumbai attack is significant. More such networks may be detected in Europe and the US in the near future.

Abandoning Terrorist Groups in Pakistan is Difficult. The terrorist groups in Pakistan are tagged as nationalist forces. For these to be abandoned, Pakistan Army has to be amenable to loosening its hold on national security strategy. At present it sees terror as a tool for calibrating relations with India, the US and the international community. Terror is seen as a "milking cow" through which American and international aid and assistance flows in. For Pakistan terrorists are foreign exchange earners. Much of this money goes for building up the Army's conventional capabilities with massive seepage in corrupt network. The US has to support the NATO troops deployed in Afghanistan logistically. With its geo-strategic location Pakistan is ideally suited for this task. Consequently, the US has very little options due to its geo-strategic compulsions.

Pakistan 'Class Interests' in Promoting Terrorism in India

(a) **Pakistan Army.** Pakistan Army has interest in maintaining hostilities with India. The Army enjoys perks and privileges that it cannot justify if differences with India are resolved, justification for their current status will get watered down and its organization may be downsized as well as downgraded in terms of its political relevance. The ISI will be out of business if they are told not to target India.

(b) **Pakistan Clergy.** The terrorist trainees are indoctrinated by the clergy. This provides clergy with gainful employment and a perverse sense of fulfillment. These people will become redundant if terrorism is stopped.

(c) **The Terrorist Groups.** Terrorism has emerged as a corporate industry. The terrorist groups in Pakistan will wither away for want of state funding or collection through religious institutions; the ISI; and from criminal connections. In case peace with India is achieved, terrorists may turn inwards on the hand that fed them. Pakistan may find it difficult to cope up with it.

CATALYSTS

India is Perceived as a Soft State

For a self respecting nation, appropriate option after the terrorist strikes on the Indian Parliament on 13 December 2001, and Mumbai carnage of 26 November 2008, would have been to take punitive action like the USA did after 11 September 2001; defend firmly against retaliation; and control escalation if so required. Irrespective of opinions on the issue, the US has not faced a repeat of 9/11, whereas

India continues to battle this scourge with recurrence of similar acts nationwide. After 1971, Pakistan has never been punished for its nefarious acts carried out in India. *Operation Parakarm* came close, but was probably never intended to go across. *Operation Vijay* in Kargil in 1999 was limited only to eviction, no punishment was inflicted.

On 16 July 2009, at Sharm el Sheikh, the joint Indo- Pakistan statement said, *"Action on terrorism should not be linked to the composite dialogue process and these should not be bracketed."* After the recent SAARC Meeting in Thimpu, Pakistan's Foreign Minister Shah Mehmood Qureshi said, " *Terrorism was a global concern that was best addressed collectively."* If we compare this to the alacrity with which Islamabad acted when Washington cracked the whip after arrest of Faizal Shahzad in New York on 08 May 2010 for terrorism, it is amazing. Within hours the police picked up suspects in Lahore for interrogation by the Federal Bureau of Investigation of the USA. The Obama Administration warned Pakistan of "Severe Consequences" if an attack of the kind attempted in 'Times Square New York' were successful and traced back to Pakistan. The reality is that when Washington talks, Islamabad listens, but when Delhi talks, Islamabad talks back.

Pakistan has hundreds of Indian Muslim modules to carry out terrorist strikes. Since the direction, training and financial support of the terrorist modules operating in India is in Pakistan, action must be taken to destroy such infrastructure. The key issue is to convince Pakistan that it will have to pay a heavy price for such acts. Shedding the tag of a soft state, vulnerable to terrorist attacks, is essential for India to rise above the mediocrity of a developing country.

Inadequate Policing

The police forces are mired with political interference, deficiency of manpower and resources. Although there has been exponential growth of many types of police forces, effective policing system is yet to emerge in the country. Militants very rarely get caught prior to inflicting casualties. Police gets activated after the incidents in most cases.

Ethos and Training of Paramilitary Forces

In view of large scale terrorism and proxy war in India, paramilitary forces need to be trained for a much higher standard of performance; provided better equipment; appropriately led; and properly commanded. However; there is a strongly held conviction among the leadership of the Home Ministry[3] and police service that paramilitary forces should be non-military in culture, ethos, and standard of training. The Mumbai carnage of 26 November 2008, and massacre of 76 CRPF *jawans* by Maoists in Chhatisgarh on 06 April 2010 are wake up calls to re-evaluate their assumptions. While re-evaluation and may be restructuring takes place, the NSAs operating in India have a high confidence level and an air of superiority on account of better training, high level of motivation and better equipment. This acts as a catalyst for better performance.

Ceasefire and Surrender policy

It has generally been noticed that as and when militant groups are cornered and the security forces have an upper hand, a lot of political pressure is brought for agreeing to ceasefire and negotiations. The announcement is generally made prematurely without proper preparatory work merely to satisfy political ends. There is generally a lack of content even in surrender policy in case it is announced. In practice it gives an opportunity to the militants to regroup and recoup and resume their activities at a later date with a vengeance.

---

[3] K Subrahmanyam, 'Where does the buck Stop?' *Times of India (New Delhi)* p18, 08 April 2010.

CONCLUSION

Countering terrorism is a holistic process. To tackle terror we need determined leaders. Shedding the tag of a country vulnerable to terrorist attacks is essential for India. The key issue is to convince Pakistan that it will have to pay a heavy price for such acts. This can be done by building comprehensive national strength and effective leadership possessing political will to use it

Session II

Non State Actors in the Indian Context

Chairman   -   Shri Ajit Doval, IPS (Retd)

Speakers   -   Shri Praveen Swami

            -    Shri E M Rammohan, IPS (Retd)

            -    Ms Vinita Priyedarshi

Experiments in Covert Warfare
Pakistan's Jihad in Jammu and Kashmir

Praveen Swami

Late on the night of September 18, 1988, a single Jammu and Kashmir Liberation Front operative named Riyaz Ahmad Sheikh arrived outside the gate of Deputy Inspector General of Police Ali Mohammad Watali. Brandishing a weapon, he loudly demanded that the officer be awakened to meet his fate. Alarmed, a sentry at Watali's gate put his .303 Lee-Enfield rifle to use. The consequence was predictable: Sheikh is now remembered as the first martyr of the ongoing jihad in Jammu and Kashmir.

Much scholarship has been devoted to the tide of history that washed Sheikh on to Watali's gates: to the collisions of Kashmiri identity and Indian nationalism; Islamism, Hindutva and secularism; Pakistan and India that, amongst other things, together make up what we sometimes called the Kashmir Problem. But in this paper, I shall focus on the gun in Sheikh's hands, not the ideas in his mind. My objective is to explore the decades-old campaign of covert warfare that Pakistan's intelligence services waged in an effort to seize Jammu and Kashmir—a campaign which placed a Kalashnikov-series assault rifle in Sheikh's hands.

Pakistan's covert services initiated what Prime Minister Jawaharlal Nehru described as an "informal war" soon after independence.[1] Its policy establishment well understood, particularly after its effort to take Jammu and Kashmir by force in 1947 failed, that its military objectives against India could not be secured through conventional tactics given the enormous resource-disparity between the adversaries. For the task of waging covert war, Pakistan's covert services were however relatively well-equipped. At Independence, the senior-most Indian official in the British Intelligence Bureau, Qurban Ali, chose Pakistani citizenship, and decamped with what material of value the departing imperial regime did not destroy. Little open source material is available on the precise impacts of Qurban Ali's actions, but one credible commentator has made clear that, in 1947, the Intelligence Bureau was in "a tragi-comic state of helplessness".[2]

Although India and Pakistan ended their first war on January 1, 1949, the police officer Surendra Nath was later to record that the cease-fire was "merely a prelude to the Pakistani efforts to grab Kashmir by other means".[3] By the spring of 1948, Pakistan had begun to use covert means to supplement its conventional offensive in Jammu and Kashmir. Police raids carried out that year led to the recovery of 643 bombs, 666 hand-grenades and 83 tins of fuses. Police investigators discovered that this materiel had been brought into Jammu and Kashmir by a Srinagar resident working for Pakistani intelligence, Salim Jehangir Khan. Pakistan's covert services also ran weapons to Hyderabad, where groups like the Islamist organisation of Kasim Rizvi had initiated armed resistance to Indian rule. Lieutenant-General Gul Hasan Khan has recorded that an unnamed "elder statesman" organised at

[1] C. Dasgupta, *War and Diplomacy in Kashmir: 1947-1948*(New Delhi: Sage Publications, 2002). 102

[2] L.P. Sen, *Slender Was the Thread* (New Delhi: Orient Longman, 1994).19

[3] [SECRET] *Report on Pakistani-Organised Subversion, Sabotage and Infiltration in Jammu and Kashmir*(Jammu and Kashmir: Criminal Investigation Department, 1966). 16

least one shipment of 0.22 calibre pistols to Hyderabad on a hired DC-3 aircraft.[4]

From 1951, Pakistani covert warfare in Jammu and Kashmir acquired sharper focus, the consequence of the fact that elections for the state's Constituent Assembly were nearing. On August 20, 1951, for example, a government-owned rest house and a bridge at Akar, in southern Kashmir, were set on fire. The group eventually held responsible for the arson were also found to have been responsible for five earlier acts of sabotage, including the burning of bridges on roads leading out of Srinagar, the destruction of a Forest Department office and the cutting of the military telephone line from Srinagar to Gulmarg. Fourteen members of the covert group that carried out the attacks were eventually tried, and nine convicted. Several Pakistani nationals – including Abbas Ali Shah, the Superintendent of Police in charge of the Criminal Investigation Department in Rawalpindi and Major Asghar Ali Shah, a military officer based at Hillan, in Pakistan-administered Kashmir – were also charged with a role in the attacks.[5] As far as I have been able to determine, this was the first legally-supported Indian charge of Pakistani state complicity in acts of terrorism in Jammu and Kashmir.

Despite India's irritation, this early covert war in Jammu and Kashmir seemed to be a low-cost and low-risk enterprise. India was, quite obviously, not going to go to war because of a few destroyed bridges of wires. Yet, to Pakistan's supporters within Jammu and Kashmir, such operations demonstrated that all was not yet lost. Soon, plans for its expansion of the jihad in Jammu and Kashmir, as its proponents and protagonists understood it to be, were pushed through Pakistan's establishment. Major-General

[4] Gul Hasan Khan, *Memoirs* (Karachi: Oxford University Press, 1993). 230-231

[5] [SECRET] *Report on Pakistani-Organised Subversion, Sabotage and Infiltration in Jammu and Kashmir* (Jammu and Kashmir: Criminal Investigation Department, 1966). 17-18

Akbar Khan, the officer who commanded Pakistan's offensive operations in 1947-1948, first provided an outline of how a 500-man covert force could be raised to target "unguarded bridges, isolated wires and unprotected transport".[6] In Khan's view, in the unlikely event that such harrying action led to war, "so much the better as this would tend to threaten the existing international peace and only then would there be reason for the United Nations again to take note of the [Kashmir] problem".[7] By Khan's account, Malik Feroze Khan Noon, who took power as Pakistan's Prime Minister in 1957, made operational these offensive plans under the command of a police officer, Mian Anwar Ali.[8]

Anti-India propaganda material began to flow across the Cease-Fire Line: and so did four covert groups, controlled from Pakistan-administered Kashmir by a Deputy Superintendent of Police, Khan Mohammad Khan. Three groups, led by Bagh Ali, Ismail and Rahim, operated in the Jammu province; two others, under the command of Jehangir Khan and Aziz Parwana, carried out operations in the Kashmir valley. Religious indoctrination played a major role in the training of this cadre. Apart from their regular military instructions, the groups' operatives received instruction from a cleric who emphasised the theological legitimacy of their enterprise. Operatives were told that the religious rights of Kashmiri Muslims had been suppressed, and that they were no longer free to offer *Namaz* prayers or celebrate festivals.[9] Apart from several explosions in public places, including a Srinagar mosque, the groups also carried out at least one targeted assassination, the murder of a Hindu-nationalist politician who

---

[6] Akbar Khan, *Raiders in Kashmir* (Islamabad: National Book Foundation, 1975). 180

[7] Akbar Khan, *Raiders in Kashmir* (Islamabad: National Book Foundation, 1975). 178

[8] Akbar Khan, *Raiders in Kashmir* (Islamabad: National Book Foundation, 1975). 181-182

[9] [SECRET] *Report on Pakistani-Organised Subversion, Sabotage and Infiltration in Jammu and Kashmir* (Jammu and Kashmir: Criminal Investigation Department, 1966). 161-164

had played a prominent role in communal violence in the Poonch area, Roopay Shah. Indian officials also charged that these groups had the support of Jammu and Kashmir's most prominent politician, Sheikh Mohammad Abdullah. The complex story of what came to be known as the Kashmir Conspiracy Case is, however, not germane to my narrative here.

What lessons can be learned from this period of covert warfare in Jammu and Kashmir? First up, the violence was terrorist in character. Bar the cutting of the Srinagar-Gulmarg telephone line, none of the targets chosen in these early acts of violence was military in character. Their purpose was not to bring down the Indian state by force, but to demonstrate Pakistani power to civil society in Jammu and Kashmir and thus influence political developments. Pakistan's covert tacticians clearly understood that the value of violence lies not in the numbers of lives that it claims, but in the theatrical impact of such action on the consciousness of its intended audiences, in this case those within Jammu and Kashmir who disputed Jammu and Kashmir's accession to India. As such, Pakistan's covert war in Jammu and Kashmir required very limited military resources. Yet, an escalatory cycle was already evident. Akbar Khan's plans had not involved assassinations or bombings of public places, and yet they took place. Once capabilities were made available to end-users, the specific forms of their use could no longer be controlled in anything other than a loose manner.

At the end of 1957, the loss of life caused by terrorism was absurdly low – and yet, the characters in the script authored by Pakistan's covert services were already starting to write their own lines.

New Doctrines and New Practices

What lessons might the strategists of Pakistan's covert war have learned from these early experiments? We have no real open-source evidence to draw upon, but no great imagination is needed to make some plausible surmises about what these might have been: there was a strong case for an enhancement of the capabilities of the jihad.

Despite the ability of Indian counter-intelligence to eventually terminate their operations, the covert groups of the 1950s had scored several notable successes. First, the covert groups had succeeded in creating political ferment in Jammu and Kashmir and adding weight to voices in the state opposed to its accession to India. Whether or not Sheikh Abdullah himself had anything to do with these covert groups, the fact is they demonstrated that a constituency, however indeterminate in size, existed for Pakistan. Second, the groups had succeeded in inflicting costs upon India, small costs but costs none the less, upon India, without pushing it to go to war. As such, the secret jihad seemed a low-cost, high-yield investment, one into which it was well worth pumping in further resources.

Third, and perhaps most important, the strategic balance between the two adversaries appeared to have been transformed with India's defeat at the hands of China in 1962. Pakistani strategists saw India as an unsustainable national project, one which would require only the slightest push before its multiple social fissures widened to the point of disintegration. In addition, some believed that India's people would prove unable to resist aggression, for "we", that is Pakistan's Muslims, "have ruled them for eight centuries – matters which cannot be wiped of the memory of the masses overnight".[10] With India demoralised by its eastern defeat, the risk of a full-blown war seemed worth taking. India's rearmament and modernisation programmes, begun after 1962, were still some way from fruition and Pakistan's supporters in Jammu and Kashmir claimed circumstances were ripe for a

---

[10] Akbar Khan, *Raiders in Kashmir* (Islamabad: National Book Foundation, 1975). 52

general insurrection.[11] Widespread anti-India protests which had broken out after the disappearance of a relic from the shrine of Hazratbal in 1964 seemed to substantiate the proposition.

Pakistan did not, contrary to popular belief, turn to planning for war at this point. Its first effort was to create a core for the insurrectionary moment it believed was imminent. In June, 1964, it threw its weight behind what came to be known to Indian counter-intelligence as 'the Master Cell', a covert group founded by Mian Ghulam Sarwar, Bashir Ahmad Kitchloo and Zafar-ul-Islam. Within months, the Master Cell had spawned a series of propaganda and military subsidiaries, as well as units to work with operatives who were launched along with the Pakistani forces who invaded Jammu and Kashmir in the summer of 1965. Although the Master Cell's structure drew on well-established traditions of revolutionary covert activity, its tactics and ideological positions were expressly Islamist in character. One key operative, Hayat Mir, tried and executed a woman for her supposed promiscuity, the first instance of a jihadi court being held in Jammu and Kashmir.[12] Social banditry, of a kind calculated to provoke communal schisms, was another favoured tactic. On one occasion, for example, a Budgam-based grocer named Raj Nath was attacked and his goods distributed amongst the local poor.[13]

In the midst of the 1965 war, the Master Cell demonstrated terror capabilities significantly more lethal than that possessed by its predecessors. Grenades, for example, were thrown in the crowded Regal Chowk and Lal Chowk areas of Srinagar;

---

[11] Rauf Klasra, 'Kashmiris "misled" Ayub in 1965 war: Gohar', *The News* (Lahore), June 2, 2005.

[12] [SECRET] *Report on Pakistani Organized Subversion, Sabotage and Infiltration in Jammu and Kashmir* (Jammu and Kashmir Government: Criminal Investigation Department, 1966). 13

[13] [SECRET] *Report on Pakistani Organized Subversion, Sabotage and Infiltration in Jammu and Kashmir* (Jammu and Kashmir Government: Criminal Investigation Department, 1966). 50

extensive urban propaganda activity was also carried. Although the war ended in a cease-fire, the Master Cell continued its campaign. By late 1965, when Indian counter-intelligence finally shut down the operation, the Master Cell was on the verge of conducting several major operations. One unit had made plans to assassinate the Jammu and Kashmir Chief Minister, G.M. Sadiq, and the Home Minister, D.P. Dhar. Another, caches of plastic explosives left behind by Pakistani forces, was preparing for a major bombing offensive. Contemporaries knew fully well what impact these resources could have had within Jammu and Kashmir:

Even without the training and the explosives, the underground cells had succeeded in creating a fairly strained situation in the valley by their acts of terrorism. Now, with the training received by two members of the Master Cell, which they would have imparted to other members, and with the availability of high explosives on such a large scale, they could have brought the normal life in the valley to a standstill.[14]

Pakistan's covert services evidently shared this assessment. Soon after the termination of the Master Cell, efforts began to put a new jihadist organization in place to consolidate its gains. In late-1966, a long-standing veteran of the secret war in Jammu and Kashmir, Ghulam Rasool Zahgir, and his Pakistani intelligence handlers began work on a new organization called al-Fatah. Zahgir's vision for al-Fatah drew heavily on the tactics of left-wing national liberation movements, notably those of the anti-colonial Front de Liberation National in Algeria. His own notion of liberation was, however, expressly Islamist in character. To Zahgir, the jihad in Jammu and Kashmir was a battle to "upkeep [sic.] our prestige

---

[14] [SECRET] *Report on Pakistani Organized Subversion, Sabotage and Infiltration in Jammu and Kashmir* (Jammu and Kashmir Government: Criminal Investigation Department, 1966). 133

Islamic honour, as Algerian Muslims have done".[15] All of this, as the scholar Stephen Cohen has noted, mirrored developments within Pakistan's armed forces. Pakistani strategists had paid close attention to debates in the United States on guerrilla warfare and Maoist notions of people's war. Where the United States sought to prevent such wars, Stephen Cohen has perceptively pointed out, Pakistan studied these "in terms of *launching* a people's war against India".[16]

To Pakistani strategists, all the necessary conditions for a people's war to succeed existed in Kashmir: in Cohen's words, "a worthy cause; difficult terrain; a determined, warlike people (the Pakistanis); a sympathetic local population (the Kashmiris); the availability of weapons and equipment; and 'a high degree of leadership and discipline to prevent (the guerrillas) from degenerating into banditry".[17] If public support had been missing in 1947-1948 or in 1965, the periodic eruption of anti-India political discontent could not have been read by Pakistani strategists as not at least offering an opportunity for its creation. While the lessons of the war of 1965 were evident – Pakistan simply could not defeat India in the battlefield, with or without the support of irregular forces – the hope clearly remained that a large-scale insurrection would alter the balance of power, at least within the limited context of Jammu and Kashmir. Zahgir believed the best way of doing this was to use limited terrorist actions to provoke reprisals by the state against "the [Kashmiri] nation as a whole,

---

[15] Ghulam Rasool Zahgir, fragments of handwritten notes maintained from November 1968 to January 1969, in [SECRET] *Report on Underground Organisation Known as al-Fatah* (Jammu and Kashmir Police: Criminal Investigation Department, 1971). 1

[16] Stephen P. Cohen, *The Idea of Pakistan* (New Delhi: Oxford University Press, 2005). 104

[17] Stephen P. Cohen, *The Idea of Pakistan* (New Delhi: Oxford University Press, 2005). 104-105

thereby creating anger and [a sense of] violation amongst the hearts of people".[18]

Al-Fatah carried out its first military operation in February, 1967, the murder of a Border Security Force constable on the Nawakadal Bridge in Srinagar. It was a minor action, but Zahgir understood the need for patience: the war against India, he recorded in his diaries, would have to involve slowly weakening the enemy, just as "a mosquito does while fighting with an elephant".[19] After this inaugural act of violence, it set up a training camp in the forests above Beerwah – using a facility first established for the Master Cell's Pakistani operatives – and began to funnel cadre for training in Pakistan. These cadre were used for a series of spectacular bank robberies, notably of the treasury of the Education Department in Pulwama and the vaults of the Jammu and Kashmir Bank's Hazratbal branch. One of the operatives who carried out this last robbery, however, was recognised and the Jammu and Kashmir Police's exceptionally competent counter-intelligence personnel soon succeeded in arresting Zahgir himself; his handler at the Pakistan High Commission in New Delhi, Zafar Iqbal Rathore, was expelled. The man who actually supervised the operation was Ali Mohammad Watali – the very officer on whose life was the first act of the ongoing jihad.

Why did al-Fatah fail? It was certainly not for want of enthusiasm or enterprise. Fazl-ul-Haq Qureshi, now a political of a certain prominence in Jammu and Kashmir, has placed on record the fact that al-Fatah had succeeded in sending 300 cadre for

---

[18] Ghulam Rasool Zahgir, handwritten notes maintained from November 1968 to January 1969, in [SECRET] *Report on Underground Organisation Known as al-Fatah* (Jammu and Kashmir Police: Criminal Investigation Department, 1971). 16

[19] Ghulam Rasool Zahgir, fragments of handwritten notes maintained fro m November 1968 to January 1969, in [SECRET] *Report on Underground Organisation Known as al-Fatah* (Jammu and Kashmir Police: Criminal Investigation Department, 1971). 1

training to Pakistan by 1971, recruiting from mosques across the countryside. Rather, Qureshi said, the real problem was that weapons were not forthcoming, "as Pakistan had decided that the time was not ripe to arm the jehadis [jihadis]".[20] From Salim Jehangir, the Pakistani agent who ran al-Fatah's training camp, Zahgir learned that large caches of sten guns did exist with which he could have armed his cadre. However, Haji Jalaluddin, the operative who held the weapons, had strict instructions not to hand them over to al-Fatah until he received authorisation from Pakistan's covert services. Had these assets been made over to al-Fatah, it is possible it would not have been forced to conduct the kinds of high-risk, low-yield operations that eventually led to its dismantling.

Pakistan's concerns in 1971, however, were focussed to the east—not on Jammu and Kashmir. India was in the process of doing to Pakistan in Bangladesh what Pakistan had sought to do in Jammu and Kashmir in 1971: cutting apart the country using a massive irregular campaign, supplemented by conventional force. In the build-up to the war of 1971, Pakistan had no interest in providing a pretext to India for going to war. In the wake of its vivisection in 1971, Pakistan would retreat from its covert war in Jammu and Kashmir for the best part of a decade. A small organisation called the National Liberation Front, two of whose cadre had hijacked an Indian Airlines aircraft to Lahore on the eve of the 1971 war, would carry on the battle alone. With few resources, and suspect in the eyes of Pakistan's covert services, the NLF would have only a negligible military impact during this period. Bar the assassination of a mid-ranking Indian diplomat, and that in London, the NLF achieved nothing of military value. Yet, the same organisation would emerge as a formidable force when the floodgates of Pakistani military resources would be opened to it in 1988-1989.

---

[20] Pradeep Thakur, *Militant Monologues* (New Delhi: Parity Paperbacks, 2003). 100

Years of Retreat

"*AZADI ka ek hi dhang,* guerrilla *jang,* guerrilla *jang*", went the anthem of the NLF: guerrilla war is the only way to freedom".

Yet, for much of its history, the organisation simply did not have the resources to translate this maxim into meaningful praxis. Formed in November 1965, just after Pakistan's defeat in the war of 1965, the NLF was born of the conviction that for the jihad in Jammu and Kashmir to be successful, it would as far as possible have to be independent of that country's military and covert services. The realisation was in part pragmatic – Pakistan's strategic weaknesses were clear to all willing to look reality in the eye, and it in any case had thrown its weight behind al-Fatah – but also driven by the ideological commitment of the NLF leadership to an independent Kashmir, not a future as part of either of South Asia's two principal powers.

In practice, the vision of an independent armed struggle proved more difficult to realise than the NLF leadership had perhaps envisaged. Its first foray into Jammu and Kashmir was betrayed. In the autumn of 1966, after two NLF units which crossed the cease-fire line had been active for barely eight weeks, their three top leaders were arrested after a firefight which claimed the life of a police officer and an operative.[21] With its founder and top ideologue, Mohammad Maqbool Butt, in jail, facing a sentence of death, the organisation went into a three year retreat. Then, in 1969, the NLF had a lucky break. A young Srinagar resident named Hashim Qureshi offered his services to the organisation towards the end of 1969, during a personal visit to Peshawar. Inspired by the September, 1970, hijacking of five aircraft by the Popular Front for the Liberation of Palestine, Qureshi and his cousin, Ashraf Qureshi, decided to stage a similar enterprise on behalf of the NLF.

---

[21] Sati Sahni, *Kashmir Underground* (New Delhi: Har Anand, 1999). 57

Much controversy has raged over the subsequent hijacking of an Indian Airlines aircraft, the Ganga, to Lahore in 1971. Some commentators have charged that Qureshi was an Indian *agent provocateur*; the hijacker himself, who now resides in Srinagar, has strenuously denied the charges, marshalling more than a small amount of persuasive evidence to his defence.[22] I shall not enter the debate here, since it is not germane to my argument. The main point was that, bereft of state sponsorship, including training and materiel, the hijacking itself turned into something of farce. All passengers were released soon after the aircraft landed in Lahore, leaving the hijackers nothing to bargain with. "We were very young", Ashraf Qureshi was to ruefully recall, "and did not realise that the passengers were more important than the aircraft".[23] What dramatic impact the affair had was soon overtaken by the India-Pakistan war that led to the creation of Bangladesh – a conflict in which India demonstrated that two could play at covert war, and that it had resources to commit which Pakistan did not.

For a decade after the 1971 war, the NLF went into decline. Much of its leadership left Pakistan-administered Kashmir, and moved to the United Kingdom. Those who attempted to join the jihad received a less-than-enthusiastic welcome in Pakistan. In May, 1973, for example, a group of students led by Syed Nazir Geelani abandoned their studies in Kashmir University and reported as volunteers at a Pakistani military post across what was now called the Line of Control.[24] There were small NLF attacks operations within Jammu and Kashmir, notably an

---

[22] Hashim Qureshi, *The Unveiling of Truth* (Lahore: Jeddojuddh Publications, 1999).

[23] Alistair Lamb, *Kashmir: A Disputed Legacy, 1846-1990* (Hertingfordsbury: Roxford Books, 1991). 292

[24] Syed Nasir Geelani, 'Ravindra Mhatre to Akhtar Bano – Blood on Our Hands', *Kashmir Images* (Srinagar), November 20, 2003

attempted bombing of parading Indian troops, but none which demonstrated any great capability. Pakistan's covert services, for their part, busied themselves in the north, fighting the pro-Moscow regime which had taken power in Kabul. In 1974, for example, Pakistan sponsored an Islamist-led covert campaign to retaliate against Afghan support for the incorporation of ethnic-Pashtun areas within its territory, which in turn had gathered momentum after the creation of Bangladesh. Without the kinds of large-scale military support available to Bangladesh insurgents, however, the Pashtun movement went nowhere.

By the mid-1980s, the NLF's operations were centred out of London. It briefly toyed with the idea of staging an attack on the 1983 summit of non-aligned states in New Delhi, but found itself without the resources to do so. Then, in January 1984, the NLF assassinated Ravindra Mhatre, a mid-ranking Indian diplomat serving in the United Kingdom. The operation was carried out even as another NLF cell considered executing another hijacking. Again, the bankruptcy of its capabilities are illustrated by the fact that training for the operation consisted of Altaf Qureshi, along with his fellow would-be hijackers Afzal Tahir and Malik Ejaz, watching a popular movie to acquaint themselves "with the new techniques in hijacking".[25] Mhatre's assassination had no real impact on the fortunes of the jihad in Jammu and Kashmir – other than that India promptly carried out the legally-sanctioned hanging of Maqbool Butt, the founder of the NLF.

Until the mid-1980s, then, the jihad in Jammu and Kashmir had passed through three distinct phases: the low-grade war which began after 1948, and culminated in the Master Cell; al-Fatah, which was the child of the study of the new people's war techniques that were being practiced in Vietnam and Algeria, and the quasi-independent operations of the Master Cell. At the core

---

[25] Hashim Qureshi, *The Unveiling of Truth* (Lahore: Jeddojuddh Publications, 1999). 44

of the successes and failures of each of these were the capabilities they were able to acquire – small arms, explosives and funds, in other words, the stuff of warfare. Of these three phases, the informal war was perhaps the most likely to succeed. Considerable military resources were committed to the operation, and it was followed by direct military intervention by Pakistan. However, India proved a stronger adversary than envisaged. The second phase set about building a more rigorous base for an insurrection, but failed again because Pakistan found itself unable to provide the resources al-Fatah needed. The NLF was stillborn, for it was starved from the outset.

Yet, this very organisation, fed with the right kinds of capabilities, was to soon emerge as the spearhead of the jihad.

The Nuclear Jihad

> "Terror", wrote the Pakistani military theoretician Brigadier SK Malik, "is not a means of imposing [a] decision upon the enemy; it is *the decision* we wish to impose upon him".[26]

In 1988, hundreds of armed jihadist cadre, equipped with weapons of a quality and quantity never seen in India before, began streaming across the Line of Control, starting a brutal war which continues to this day. It is not my purpose here to provide an account of the current stage of the jihad in Jammu and Kashmir, but rather to examine how this fourth phase came about – the circumstances which made it possible for Pakistan to increase the capabilities of its covert forces to unprecedented levels. Many political explanations have been offered for why events took the form they did in 1988. The rigging of elections in 1987, the economic and social frustrations of young Kashmiris, and the undermining of the institutions of democracy in India, all these

---

[26] SK Malik, *The Quranic Conception of War* (New Delhi: Himalayan Books, 1986). 59

together offer insight into the strains that underpinned the extraordinary violence we have since witnessed. However, as our survey of the earlier phases of the jihad shows, conditions had always existed in which large numbers of young people were willing to fight, and to die, for their vision of Jammu and Kashmir's future.

Why, then, did this particular phase of war take the unimaginably horrific form it did?

Provoked by the Soviet Union's intervention in Afghanistan, the United States and its west Asian allies began to funnel enormous flows to weapons and funds to the Islamist resistance in Afghanistan. By as early as 1987, at least 80,000 mujahideen had been trained by Pakistan's covert services; in that year alone, 65,000 tons of arms and munitions, including high-technology anti-armour and anti-aircraft missiles, were made over to forces battling Soviet and Afghan forces.[27] Pakistan, acutely aware of India's long-standing alliance with the Soviet Union, made the entirely rational decision of exerting pressure on its eastern neighbour early on. By 1983, Pakistan's covert services began to funnel light weapons, notably AK-series assault rifles, to groups fighting for the creation of Sikh theocratic state in the Indian province of Punjab.[28] In past years, this threat would have provoked a conventional reprisal, and that, in 1986, is exactly what India signalled its willingness to execute. In July that year, India initiated Operation Brasstacks, a massive exercise intended to demonstrate its capability to wage a full-blown war against Pakistan.

---

[27] Mohammad Yusaf and Mark Adkin,*Afghanistan: The Bear Trap* (Havertown: Casemate, 2001). 111, 98

[28] For a discussion of the mechanics of this aid, see Paveen Swami, 'Failed Threats and Flawed Fences: India's Military Responses to Pakistan's Proxy War', in *The India Review* Vol. 3 No. 2 (London: Frank Cass, 2004).

Pakistani military strategists, well aware that exercises had been used in the past to disguise war mobilisation, responded with moving up its reserves into positions that threatened key Indian cities in Punjab. As India's strike formations were too far away to immediately respond to this threat, troops were airlifted to defend these cities. An escalatory cycle was well underway when Pakistan's Minister of State for Foreign Affairs, Zain Noorani, conveyed what the Indian Ambassador in Islamabad took to be a nuclear threat.[29] A more specific warning of Pakistan's new nuclear capabilities was conveyed to the Indian journalist Kuldip Nayar, on January 28, 1997. The threat worked. Confronted with an irregular war in 1965, India has responded with a full-scale counter offensive. This time around, it could not. From after the end of Operation Brasstacks, levels of violence in Punjab registered a steady increase until 1990-1991, with levels of violence in the worst periods far exceeding the worst seen in Jammu and Kashmir. Within Jammu and Kashmir itself, levels of violence again escalated after 1998, a development closely related to the capabilities of terrorist groups [see table on page 96].

Indian commentators have, in general, fought shy of linking the events of Operation Brasstacks with Pakistan's emerging nuclear capabilities. General K Sundarji, who commanded India's army at the time, displayed no such squeamishness. He candidly admitted that Pakistan's nuclear assets, however rudimentary they might have been at that time, had removed from the menu of Indian responses the possibility of "launching a bold offensive across the Punjab border".[30] Put another way, India could no longer take recourse to its "stated, avowed strategy of reacting in the plains

---

[29] *From Surprise to Reckoning: Kargil Review Committee Report*(New Delhi: Government of India Press, 1999). 159

[30] Devin Hagerty , 'Nuclear Deterr ence in South Asia' , *International Security*, Winter 1995-1996, V ol. 20 No . 3, cited in Pra vin Sawhney, *The Defence Mak eover* (New Delhi: Sage Publications, 2002). 350

conventionally". Sundarji displayed a sound grasp of theory. As Sumit Ganguly and Devin Hagerty have argued, "nuclear weapons deter war not through the classical modalities identified by deterrence theorists—relative capabilities, demonstrated resolve, nuclear doctrines, escalation dominance and pointed threats— but through the fact of their existence and the accompanying possibility that they might be used at all".[31] Pakistan may or may not have used nuclear weapons in the event of a war – but India was deterred by the very possibility that it might have.

South Asia's crude nuclear equilibrium – an equilibrium founded on the fact that India, wisely or otherwise, did not wish to chance the risk of one bomb hitting one city – was to shape the course of events to come. Successive crisis would haunt the course of the nuclear jihad. Soon after the Brasstacks crisis, Pakistan's covert services opened dialogue with the NLF, now renamed the Jammu Kashmir Liberation Front. Now certain that India could not respond to Pakistani provocation with all out war, as it had done in 1965, the floodgates could be opened for the resources made available by the end of the Afghan jihad. Periodic crisis would haunt the course of the nuclear jihad. In 1990, for example, as the jihad began to spiral towards the climactic levels of violence that would be witnessed in the middle of the decade, Pakistan initiated military manoeuvres that provoked an Indian counter-mobilisation. We have, hopefully, seen the last of these crisis in 2002, after which Pakistan has ratcheted back its support to jihadist groups by some measure, a fact demonstrated in declining levels of violence. In 2007, Jammu and Kashmir saw less than 1,000 fatalities in a year: figures that, in pre-capital terms,

---

[31] Sumit Ganguly and Devin T. Hagerty, *Fearful Symmetry: India-Pakistan Crises in the Shadow of Nuclear Weapons* (New Delhi: Oxford University Press, 2000). 129

are not dissimilar to homicide levels registered in the recent past in the United States of America.[32]

	Terrorists Killed	Civilians Killed	Indian Forces Killed	Acts of Violence+
1990	550	1000	155	4211
1991	844	906	173	3780
1992	819	1069	189	4842
1993	1310	1057	198	5273
1994	1596	1069	200	5851
1995	1332	1202	237	5946
1996	1209	1424	189	5023
1997	1075	1030	216	3437
1998	999	967	268	2940
1999	1082	937	407	3073
2000	1520	942	482	3091
2001	2020	1098	613	4536
2002	1707	1050	539	4038
2003	1494	836	384	3401
2004	976	733	330	2565
2005	917	556	244	1990
2006	591	410	182	1667
2007	472	170	122	1092
Statistical Report, Fortnight Ending January 14, 2008 (Srinagar: Jammu and Kashmir Police HQ, 2008). Page 13, 14)				
+ Sum of incidents of grenade throwing, IED explosions arsons, rocket attacks, random fire,cross-fire, arms snatching, kidnapping, hanging and miscellaneous acts of violence				

[32] Jammu and Kashmir has a population of 7718,700 [Jammu and Kashmir Government, http://jammukashmir.nic.in/profile/facts.htm]. Violence-related fatalities in 2007 were therefore 9.89 per 100,000 population. The peak United States homicide rate, in 1980, was 10.2 [United States Department of Justice, http://www.ojp.usdoj.gov/bjs/homicide/hmrt.htm]

Some Conclusions

For a number of reasons, though, it would be ill-advised to be sanguine about the future. First, while violence in Jammu and Kashmir has declined in recent years, jihadist groups with India have become increasingly active. Organizations like the Indian Mujahideen, born of decades of anti-Muslim communal violence, have deep ties with Pakistan's intelligence services as well as jihadist groups like the Lashkar-e-Taiba.[33] As such, the diminishing levels of violence in Jammu and Kashmir could conceivably be offset by the increasing intensity of terrorism elsewhere in India.

Second, it is far from clear if Pakistan's military and intelligence services have in fact made a determination to terminate covert warfare directed at India and elsewhere.

Of course, Pakistan has several excellent reasons to make a strategic u-turn. First, the jihadist groups committed to fighting India, in and outside Jammu and Kashmir, also pose a threat to the Pakistani state. Moreover, as the economist Akbar Zaidi has documented, has yielded little. The two-decade old nuclear jihad has seen Pakistan's decline relative to that of India, the precise opposite of the outcome its architects had presumably hoped for.[34]

But a mass of recent media commentary suggests otherwise; at least one book asserts that the Pakistan army, at its highest levels, continues to retain close links with jihadist groups.[35] If so, this would suggest that the decline in violence in Jammu and

---

[33] For an account of these groups, see 'India's and its invisible jihad' in Satish Kumar (ed.), *India's National Security Annual Review, 2008* (New Delhi: KW Publishers, 2008). Also see'The Well-Tempered Jihad: the politics and practice of post-2002 Islamist terrorism in India', in 'Contemporary South Asia' Volume 16, Issue 3 (September 2008).

[34] S. Akbar Zaidi, *Pakistan's Economic & Social Development* (New Delhi: Rupa, 2004). 54-55

[35] David Sangar, *The Inheritance* (London: Bantam, 2009).

Kashmir is largely a tactical measure driven by the risk of war, rather than a reversal of course. Indeed, in the summer of 2008, Pakistani and Indian troops regularly traded fire on the Line of Control, threatening a ceasefire which went into place in 2002.[36]

Pakistan's covert services also have a deep ideological commitment to the notion of the jihad as a core obligation of the state itself. Zia-ul-Haq placed Islam at the core of the Pakistan Army's *raison d'etre*. Its involvement in Islamist causes was no longer merely tactical; it was an ideological imperative. This use of Islam to legitimize the state's use of coercive means was not, of course, new. General Yahya Khan had, at a late stage of the East Pakistan crisis, described enemy forces as *kaffirs*, or unbelievers, and his own troops as *mujaheddin*, or soldiers of Islam. The notion of jihad, similarly, fed and informed each successive phase of covert warfare in Jammu and Kashmir. Now, however, Islam was no longer merely a faith, appeals to which could be made for opportunistic purposes. It was firmly enshrined as an institutional ideology. Courses in Islam became part of the curriculum at officer-training colleges. Soon, religion began to express itself as a key component of military doctrine. Sub-conventional warfare, in the hands of ideologists like Brigadier SK Malik, was seen as an especially appropriate form of combat. Terror, in particular, was seen as having religious sanction. "This position may not be publicly flaunted", Stephen Cohen has recently noted, "but it is widely held in the army".[37]

Third, the prospect remains that Islamist groups may capture the Pakistani state itself.

---

[36] Praveen Swami, 'LoC skirmish sparks fears of bloody summer', *The Hindu* (Chennai), May 20, 2009 . Online at http://www.hindu.com/2008/05/20/stories/2008052060870100.htm

[37] Stephen P. Cohen, *The Idea of Pakistan* (New Delhi: Oxford University Press, 2005).

119

Whether the Nuclear Jihad will mark the final phase of Pakistan's covert war in Jammu and Kashmir, or just a prelude to a new and even more macabre confrontation, therefore remains to be seen.

The Heart of our Darkness

Shri EN Rammohan

Waking up to Naxalism

The killing of 74 Central Reserve Police Force (CRPF) soldiers on the wee hours of April 6, 2010 at Chintalnar near Dantewara in the Bastar area of Chattisgarh state seems to have finally woken up the Indian establishment to the fact that while they have been obsessing with economic growth and India's place in the world, the country's hinterland is witnessing an awakening of another kind. A raging insurgency, with its epicenter in the *Adivasi*[1] homelands of central India, is threatening to engulf at least a quarter of India's 590 districts. It would not be very far off the mark to state that over 200 million people now live in areas where insurgents of some kind or the other are in armed conflict with the Indian State. It's not by coincidence that in much of this area, there is a sizable tribal population. Much of the insurgency can now be attributed to Naxalism, probably making it the last communist ideology inspired insurgency in the world. But now the geographical scale dwarfs every such conflict the world

[1] Although terms such as *atavika* (Sanskrit for *forest dwellers*), *vanvasi* or *girijan* (*hill people*) are also used for the tribes of India, *Adivasi* carries the specific meaning of being the original and autochthonous inhabitants of a given region, and was specifically coined for that purpose in the 1930s. Over a period of time, unlike the terms "aborigines" or "tribes", the word "*adivasi*" has also developed a connotation of past autonomy, which was disrupted during the colonial period in India and has not been restored. Opposition to usage of the term is varied, and it has been argued that the "original inhabitant" contention is based on dubious claims and that the adivasi - non-adivasi divide that is created is artificial. It should also be noted that in Northeast India, the term Adivasi applies only to the Tea tribes imported from Central India during colonial times, while all tribal groups refer collectively to themselves by using the English word "tribes". Thus, generally speaking the term Adivasi is used to refer to the tribal communities in Hindu dominant areas.

has known save the Chinese civil war that finally ended with Mao Zedong's victory. China has moved on a long way since then, and almost certainly China's present Chairman no longer inspires the Naxalites, as the first Chairman did.[2]

But the Indian *Adivasi* regions have been troubled much before the advent of Naxalism or Maoism, as some prefer it. The Naxalite leadership, which is mostly non-*Adivasi*, has however managed to superimpose its ideological orientation on the long prevalent disaffection of the tribal people. While the Maoists have managed to exploit the tribal unrest over their exploitation and the destruction of their traditional homelands, it would be wrong of the Indian State to tar the *Adivasi* unrest as naxalism.

When the troubles first erupted in the predominantly tribal village of Naxalbari[3] and began spreading to other areas in West Bengal, a popular slogan then was "China's Chairman is our Chairman". It may not have fired the minds of the rural masses, but it caught on in the university campuses all over the country. Many students of Delhi's elite St.Stephens College even went underground to fight for the

---

[2] From the Naxalite groups who held that China was the center of the world revolution, a substantial number now have gone over to the position that the CPC has betrayed world revolution. The CPC's authoritative documents produced in the sixth plenum of the CC, the eleventh and twelfth congresses, have become for them the bedrock of revisionism and betrayal of Mao Zedong thought. The blind and dogmatic adherence to Mao Zedong thought as the essence of Marxism-Leninism of the epoch- a position that the CPC itself does not maintain now-is the key to the ideological disarray these groups have reached **The Marxist**; Volume: 3, No. 1; January- Mar ch 1985.

[3] During the mid 1960s Charu Mazumdar and Kanu Sanyal organized an ultra leftist faction in CPI (M) in northern Bengal. In 1967, a militant peasant uprising took place in Naxalbari, led by the Mazumdar-Sanyal group. This group would later become known as the Naxalites. The same year, Mazumdar and Sanyal broke away and formed the All India Co-ordination Committee of Communist Revolutionaries (AICCCR), which in turn founded the Communist Party of India (Marxist –Leninist) in 1969, with Mazumdar as i ts General Secretary.

Naxalbari is the name of a village and a region in northern part of the state of   West Bengal. Naxalbari comes under the jurisdiction of Darjeeling district with its sub divisional headquarter at Siliguri. The stretch of land, where Naxalbari is situated, lies on the Terai region at the base of the Himalayas. To the west of Naxalbari, across the border river Mechi lies Nepal. The entire stretch of the land surrounding Naxalbari is covered by farmlands, tea estates and forests and small villages, consists of an area of 121 km². The large villages in the region are Buraganj, Hatighisha, Phansidawa and Naxalbari.

revolution.[4] But they soon, like their compatriots from Kolkata's elite Presidency College, discovered that revolution was not a dinner party[5], or even a seminar.

If the Stephanians soon came back after discovering that they did not have it in them to stay the hard course nor an appetite for spilling blood, others and more often than not far less privileged, showed that they had in them "right stuff" and the reason for taking recourse to armed action and the violent overthrow of the state. The Naxalbari uprising in West Bengal in 1967 inspired several young Communists in the remote hilly and forested district of Srikakulam[6] in Andhra Pradesh (AP), which abuts the equally remote southeastern corner of Orissa, and they gradually turned to the politics of agrarian revolution.

The Srikakulam Communists sent Nagabhushan Patnaik[7] and Chowdhury Tejeswara Rao to Calcutta in October 1968, to hold talks

---

[4] Contemporary insiders put the number of core Naxal's in the college at the height of militancy at no more than 30 — not a big figure, but by most accounts, the single largest Maoist presence in all DU institutions. In 1968, history student Arvind Narain Das had run for president of the college student's body elections on an openly Naxal platform. He won. "We were ready to storm hea ven," Dilip Simeon, a leading member of the group , was to write later. Times have moved since. Awadhesh Sinha is additional chief secretary in the Maharashtra government. Das, Ray and Simeon went on to do their PhDs. Das, a journalist and sociologist, died in 2000. He was 52. Ray teaches at Delhi School of Economics. Simeon joined Ramjas College as a teacher in 1974. In the '80s, he was attacked brutally while leading an agitation. He is now a senior esearch fellow at Nehru Library. Rajiv Kumar did his DPhil from Oxford and is director of ICRIER a leading government supported rightwing economics thinktank.

[5] "A re volution is not a dinner part y, or wri ting an essa y, a painting a picture, or doing embroidery; it cannot be so refined, so leisurely and gentle, so temperate, kind, courteous, restrained and magnanimous. A revolution is an insurrection, an act of violence by which one class o verthrows another." – from Chairman Mao's Little Re d Book.

[6] Srikakulam town is the headquarters ofSrikakulam district in northeastern Andhra Pradesh. With the same name there is a "Srikakulam Assembly constituency" and a "Srikakulam Parliament Consti tuency'". Srikakulam municipal ity. Srikakulam w as f ormerly cal led as Gulshanabad (Garden city) during Muslim rule and was headquarter of Muslim fauzdars. The British colonial rulers renamed it as Chicacole. After independence, it was renamed as Srikakulam.

[7] " The very name, Nagabhushan Patnaik symbolizes the revolutionary spirit of the Naxalbari and the Srikakulam armed struggle. A senior politburo member of the undivided CPI (M-L), Comrade Patnaik was sentenced to death in connection with five murder cases. Later it was commuted to life sentence. After the disintegration of the original CPI (M-L), Comrade

with Charu Mazumdar. On their return, the newly formed Srikakulam district coordination committee convened a secret meeting where it was resolved that an armed struggle should be launched immediately. Guerilla squads were formed in the plains as well as in the hills of Srikakulam, with the objective of overthrowing the government and establishing a 'people's democratic dictatorship led by the proletariat."

The guerilla movement took off with the forcible harvesting of crops from the land of a rich landlord. On November 25, 1968 something more significant happened in the hill tracts of Parvatipuram. Around 250 tribal people armed with bows and arrows and spears, and led by the legendary peasant organizer, Vempatapu Sathyanarayana[8] and Nagabhushan Patnaik, raided the house of a landlord and took possession of rice and other foodgrains that he had hoarded. They also seized documents, promissory notes and other records that had bound the tribal peasants to the landlord, who was also a moneylender. Several such actions followed in

---

Nagabhushan criticized the central line of the CPI (M-L). He was one of the signatories of the famous 'Jail Letter' that was based on Zhou Enlai's 11 Point Suggestions. In his later years, comrade Patnaik joined the Liberation faction, and became one of its polit- bureau members. He advocated the utilization of the parliamentary rostrum in a Leninist fashion in direct contrast to the boycottist nature of the undivided CPI (M-L). On 9th October, 1998, Comrade Patnaik died at a priv ate hospi tal in Chennai due to r enal f ailure." POSTED **BY CPI (M-L) - THE UNFINISHED REVOLUTION** http://imp-personalities.blogspot.com/ His death inspired the poet laureate of armed struggle, Sri Sri to write: "The white man then called you Bhagat Singh /The black man now calls you Naxalite/ Everyone will tomor- row call you the morning star, /Inquilab, Inquilab, Inquilab zindabad!"

[8] **Vempatapu Sathyanarayana** (Satyam) w as a school teacher, member of sev eral I n- dian Communist organizations, and a leader of the Srikakulam Peasant Uprising of 1967, along with another schoolteacher Adhibatla Kailasam. They had started the "land to tiller" movement in Andhra Pradesh, which later spread to Koraput and Malkangiri districts in Orissa. Sathyanarayana joined the (CPI (ML)) through the All India Coordination Commit- tee of Communist revolutionaries (AICCCR). He became a member of the Central Organiz- ing Committee of the CPI (ML) in 1969. Later , he became a member of the new Central Committee that was elected in the first party congress with Charu Mazumdar as its Gen- eral S ecretary. He was also the S ecretary of the Srikakulam District Committee of the party. His small booklet on Srikakulam P easant Armed Upsurge details the natur e of Naxalite influence in the early phases of 1969 and 1970 in Andhra Pradesh. It is a common belief among the Naxalite ranks, that he was killed together with Adhibatla Kailasam in a fake encounter in Srikakulam by the Andhra Pradesh police under the prior order of the state government around 10-11 of July 1970.

Srikakulam.[9] However, by the mid 1970's the Srikakulam movement was completely crushed. More than 300 of its activists were killed in "encounters". But the fires of revolution were not to be easily doused down.

The CPI (ML) only regrouped and spread to other parts of Andhra Pradesh where we have seen periodic recrudescence. The Naxalites made several dramatic strikes in the thickly forested districts of Telangana such as Adilabad, Karimnagar and Warangal during the Emergency. In September 1976 a group of Naxalites attacked the house of a powerful landlord and Congress leader, GV Pitamber Rao, in Tappalpur village in Adilabad district. Pitamber Rao escaped but the shock of the audacious attack is said to have caused a heart attack and he died a few days later. Less than two months later on November 7, a Naxalite squad led by Kondapalli Sitaramiah, later the founder of the Peoples War Group and Muppalla Laxman Rao, presently General Secretary of the CPI (ML) once again attacked the Pitamber Rao house and killed his sons, GV Subhash and Dr. Sampat Rao. The eldest brother, Sreenivas Rao, who looked after the family's lands and businesses, and who the attackers intended victim, was fortuitously away at the family owned cinema theatre. Subhash was my classmate at Nizam College in Hyderabad and captained the cricket, basketball and hockey teams. He had little to do with the family estate in the village. The few visits were in the company of his friends like the cricketer Mansur Ali Khan Pataudi when they went out poaching on jeeps with spotlights and high-powered rifles.[10] On that fateful day, Subhash expressly went to the

---

[9] For a succinct and brief history of the Naxalbari and Srikakulam Uprisings see " **Human Rights in India: Police Killings and Rural Violence in Andhra Pradesh"** for Human Rights Watch by Patricia Grossman.

[10] **Mansur Ali Khan Pataudi** is an inveterate poacher and finally the law seemed to catch-up with him. On June 6, 2005 he was charged under sections 9, 39 and 51 of the Wildlife Protection Act 1972 for killing an endangered blackbuck. The maximum sentence for this kind of offence is seven years in prison. Police also recovered two guns and 50 cartridges from the car after it was stopped in a routine police check in Jhajjar on Friday night But as can well be expected Pataudi still runs free and can be seen regularly on TV commenting on cricketing matters, and is a high official in the Indian Premier League (IPL). Earlier in 1997

village to take part in the obsequies of a close relative. His pregnant wife, Vani, was also with him. The Naxalites came looking for his brother Srinivasa Rao, who used to assist the father in the village. Fortuitously for him, Srinivasa Rao was at the family owned cinema theatre when the Naxalites attacked the house. The September attack apparently did make the family more circumspect. Their connections and influence probably lulled them and did not keep them from going to the village. Besides a Velama[11] kinsman, Jalagam Vengala Rao was the Chief Minister and the state government had even posted a police picket in the village to provide the Pitamber Rao household with protection. Another Velama kinsman , the state's powerful DIG of Intelligence, K Vijayarama Rao, later Director of the CBI and minister in the Chandrababu Naidu cabinet, belonged to the neighboring district of Karimnagar. Despite this the Naxalite squad attacked the house and hacked down all the male members present with knives and axes. They took away the weapons in the house and disappeared into the forests. The Tappalpur raids sent a shock wave throughout the state and were seen as a turning point for the movement in Andhra Pradesh.[12]

The Tappalpur raids captured the imagination of educated youth and communist cadres all over the state. Soon after the Naxalite leaders involved in the "Tappalpur raids" were able to form the "Coordination Committee" which was later rechristened as Peoples War Group. The PWG merged with Bihar's Maoist Communist Centre

---

he and his wif e Sharmila Tagore reportedly shot some 100 migr atory birds in K ashmir's Hokersar wetland. No case was filed supposedly because they had sought and got permission for the hunt. They were in Hok ersar at the inv itation of F arooq Abdul lah, the then chief minister of Jammu and K ashmir. Sharmi la Tagore is now Chairperson of the Fil m Censor Board.

[11] Velama is one of the feudal lord castes or social groups in AP state. They ruled in parts of Andhra, Tamil Nadu, Vidarbha and all of Telangana during 14th and 15th centuries and some parts of Andhra till 19th century. Velama's are considered one of the most powerful communities in Andhra Pradesh.

[12] After over three decades, the police have re-opened the sensational case and arrested a senior Maoist leader from W est Bengal, T usharkanth Bh attacharya, and produced him before a local court in Adilabad on Nov ember 3, 2007.

(MCC) to become CPI (Maoists) in October 2004. In 1978 the newly formed Congress(I) swept the elections to the state assembly defeating the Janata Party led in the state by S. Jaipal Reddy and the ruling Congress faction led by the incumbent Chief Minister, J Vengala Rao.

The Indira wave saw the induction of Dr. M Channa Reddy as Chief Minister. The new Chief Minister held out an olive branch to the Naxalites, and initiated talks, but soon it was clear that the only intention of the Naxalites was to use the cease-fire period to regroup and reorganize. The AP Home Minister, MM Hashim, began a Track II dialogue with Naxal representatives and I took part in some of the meetings. The dialogue collapsed when the underground's representatives began to threaten the interlocutors to ensure that the cessation of operations was extended. The lull of the cease-fire allowed them to expand their cells in the Osmania and Andhra Universities. Many idealistic youth joined the movement, and unlike the upper class lads from St.Stephens and Presidency, these young people stayed the course and many even lost their lives. The intelligence wing of the AP Police was also reporting the setting up of bases in towns like Davangere in Karnataka and Dharmapuri in Tamil Nadu.

The Tappalpur raids had sent a wave of fear among the PWD, forest and excise contractors, many of them Congress (I) leaders, and Naxal coffers began to swell. Money, they say, is the mother's milk of politics, revolutionary or otherwise. The PWG also began a campaign to annihilate other Naxalite factions.[13] During this period the PWG also began extending its organization into the tribal areas

---

[13] "In one of his most celebrated classics, Lenin showed how left adventurist trends emerged in course of struggle against right opportunism during the formative period of communist parties in different countries ('Left-wing' Communism – An Infantile Disorder) at the end of the second decade of the 20th century. He saw this as a normal teething trouble ("infantile disorder") that could lead to catastrophic consequences unless cured in time. A similar phenomenon was to be observed in our country too during the formative years of the CPI (ML)." 'Maoism', State and the Communist Movement in India' ; h ttp://www.cpiml.org/liberation/year_2010/feb_10/article.html

of the neighboring states of Maharashtra, Madhya Pradesh and Orissa. Kondapalli Sitaramiah emerged as the charismatic leader and ideologue of the CPI (ML). But like Robespierre, Sitaramiah too was consumed by the revolution and the party that he built later expelled him.[14]

The Naxalites had greater success in the tribal areas of the neighboring states, where the depredations of outsiders, whether forest and excise contractors or government officials, had resulted in widespread discontent among the tribal people. The support base of the PWG swelled. Medical students from the Andhra Medical College, Guntur, and engineering students from the Regional Engineering College at Warangal now joined the Osmania University recruits. Like all such revolutionary movements, the cachet that went with being a revolutionary began to also attract lumpen elements, the type that would have otherwise joined the Youth Congress or the

---

[14] **Kondapalli Sitaramiah**, at a young age, joined the communists. He went on to become the Krishna district Secretary of the CPI. His CPI uni t was active during the Telangana Rebellion. When the CPI was divided in 1964, Sitaramiah withdrew from political life. He began working as a Hindi teacher at F atima S chool in Warangal. In Warangal he befriended KG Sath yamurthy. B oth men joined the Communist P arty of I ndia (Marxist Leninist). Sitaramiah became a member of the Andhra Pradesh State Committee of CPI (ML).When the CPI (ML) was torn by internal strife, Sitaramiah joined the Central Organizing Committee of the Communist Party of India (Marxist Leninist) in 1972. In August 1974, the Andhra Pradesh State Committee of COC, CPI (ML) was organized, with Sitaramiah as one of its three members. On Apri l 26, 1977 Sit aramiah was arrested in Nagpur, when police caught him with weapons in a vehicle. He was released on bail, but absconded and went underground. In 1977 he broke away from COC, CPI (ML). On April 22, 1980 he founded the CPI (ML) P eoples War. On January 2, 1982 he was arr ested in Hyderabad's Begumpet Railway Station, when waiting to board a train to Mumbai. On January 4, 1984 he managed to escape from the prisoner's wing of the Osmania Hospital.

Following an internal dispute, which ended with the expulsion of K.G. Sathyamurthy (number 2 in the party ranks) and Byreddy Sathyanarayana Reddy (militia commander in Khammam district), Sitaramiah's hold over the party strengthened. Sathyamurthy had begun questioning the Maoist character of the party, on the lines of Deng Xiaoping. Reddy had opposed Sathy amurthy's ouster. In 1991, Sit aramiah himself was ousted from the party he founded. In 1993, police caught him in his home village. After few years in prison,he was acquitted and released on humanitarian grounds. During his final years, he abstained from political activity. He suffered from Parkinson's disease. Kondapalli Sitaramiah died in his granddaughter's house in Vijayawada on April 12, 2002. He was 87 years old. His wife Koteswa ramma and two gr anddaughters, V. Anuradha and G. Sudha, survived him. Funeral services were arr anged the next day. According to press reports, only a handful of people turned up.

youth wings of the other major parties. Since then the Naxalites have gone from strength to strength. The Hindustan Times of 3 January 2007 has done an excellent job of chronologically summarizing the various phases of the many hues of Naxalism since 1948.[15]

Even mainstream political parties have found it expedient to seek Naxalite support from time to time for narrow political advantage, by pandering to them and offering them concessions on coming to power. It is also believed that often support was purchased with cash. Several companies with large investments in forest-based industries also began to pay for protection. Companies often do this and we have evidence of how even India's largest business house, the Tata's, were paying off ULFA terrorists in Assam.[16] Extortion is commonplace now in Naxal areas.[17] In the run up to the 1983 elections to the Andhra Pradesh state assembly, the film actor NT Rama who was leading his recently formed Telugu Desam Party, dramatically declared himself an ally of the Naxalites. He even campaigned using the theme that they were "true patriots, who have been misunderstood by the ruling classes."[18] Almost a decade later

---

[15] http://www.hindustantimes.com/News-Feed/nm2/History-of-Naxalism/225549/Article1-6545.aspx

[16] Outlook; **September 29, 1997; "A Suspect Brew:** Life in terrorism-ridden Assam was bad enough. With a hostile state, the tea leaves bode more ill." By Nitin Gokhale and Soutik Biswas

[17] "Many of the kidnappings were related to extortions. On 19 June 2006, the CPI (ML) Pratighatana cadres abducted senior General Manager of the Nagarjuna Cements Limited, V.V. Rama Raju and hiscolleague Galib Saheb from the factory premises in Kadimpothavaram in G. Konduru mandal in Vijayawada district. The abductors demanded Rs 1 crore as ransom. However, they were reportedly set free following police operations. While V.V. Rama Raju was released on 21 June 2006, Mr. Galib was released the next day. According to the police, irrigation contractors in Naxal affected districts like Warangal and Karimnagar had to pay 2-3% of their total contract amount to the Maoists. On 3 April 2006, the police reportedly recovered Rs 50 lakhs from Jupally Raghupathi Rao, the upa-sarpanch of Kudikilla village in Kollapur mandal, and Yeruvaka Shivashankar, a site engineer of VARKS Engineer Groups, who were allegedly taking the money collected from the sub-contractors of the Kalwakurthy irrigation project to be paid to the Naxalites as extortion." **3b of the Indian Human Rights Report, 2007** of the Asian Human Rights centre, New Delhi.

[18] "The politics has been played earlier too. In 1982, N.T. Rama Rao played it with consummate skill. He called the Naxalites true patriots who had been misunderstood by the ruling classes. M. Chenna Reddy, Congress CM, acted no differently. In 1989, he, too, declared

during his second innings as Chief Minister he lifted the ban on left-wing extremism in the hope of once again associating himself with the movement's political popularity. This worked out quite well for his party due to the pockets of influence the Naxalites had in several districts.

Pandering often is a matter of minimizing the government's response to insurgent threats, either to acquire time for political enhancements or to reduce threats to officials' personal security. Prior to 2004, the Congress Party in Andhra Pradesh pledged to hold discussions with rebels if its candidates were elected. The party's pledge was a tacit agreement that while talks or negotiations were ongoing, the officials would halt counter-insurgency operations, thereby providing a recovery period for the insurgents. The Naxalites also announced their ceasefire and permitted officials to campaign in the insurgent-held areas. The rebels effectively used the suspension of counter-insurgency operations and the resulting ceasefire to recruit and consolidate their position by moving openly among the population. The Congress Party did not actively support the Maoist insurgents' ideals, but did indicate it would minimize any counter-insurgency operations in return for electoral support.[19] This it did. Soon after assumption of office in 2004, the Rajasekhara Reddy government began talks with the Naxalite leadership. A tacit ceasefire was put in place. This period lasted for exactly six months till December 16 that year. The Naxalites, as in the past, used this interregnum to attempt expansion into newer areas and the police used it to gather information and reorganize their forces to effectively tackle the extremists. Suddenly Rajasekhara Reddy, who during his long campaign for political power promised to talk to the Naxalites

---

that Naxalites were patriots. When Chief Minister N. Chandrababu Naidu adopted a firm approach against Naxalites, it was Rajasekhar Reddy's turn to appease them. In other states, too, political parties and leaders have not hesitated to arrive at an understanding with the Naxalites. " **www.hindustantimes.com/News-Feed/...is.../Article1-209723.aspx**

[19] **COIN in the Real World**   by David R. Haines; H ttp://www.carlisle.army.mil/usawc/Parameters/08winter/haines.pdf.

about the "people's problems", shifted tack and began saying: "where is the need to talk to the Naxalites about peoples problems?" He made it clear that he was only willing to talk to them about surrender.[20] Soon after the AP Police resumed operations against them and many of the prominent Naxalite leaders were killed in "encounters" – some real and some staged. The renewed and relentless pressure forced most of the Andhra naxal cadres to migrate to Maharashtra, Chattisgarh and Orissa. Many others surrendered and soon found that the vocational skills acquired in the underground had plenty of takers in India's fast globalizing market economy. Many former Naxalites are now collection agents for private agencies employed by banks like ICICI and HDFC, who lent huge sums as vehicle loans. In recent days cell phone companies have also taken recourse to collection agents. Debt collection now is an organized business and several sons of senior police officers now own successful companies and offer gainful employment to former Naxalites.[21] While the Naxal movement derived its name from a little West Bengal village, its Andhra Pradesh, that is its real home now, and which provides it with leadership and ideological sustenance.

On December 20, 2007 India's Prime Minister formally declared war on the Naxalite insurgency when he addressed a high level conference on internal security consisting Chief Ministers, Police and Intelligence chiefs, top civil servants and representatives of most political parties. Since then the Prime Minister has been using every available platform to call for the "crushing" of the Naxalites. [22]

---

[20] **Naxalites in Andhra Pradesh: Have We Heard the Last of the Peace Talks? by K Balagopal (The Economic and Political Weekly of**March 26 – April 01, 2005);Http;/ /www.epw.in/epw/uploads/articles/341.pdf

[21] 13 Oct 2003 **...** Some of the **surrendered Naxalites** have turned into a gang of criminals leading the land mafia and extortion rackets, especially in Hyderabad   **...** www.tribuneindia.com/2003/20031013/edit.htm

[22] Admitting that Naxal groups have succeeded in enlarging their base, Prime Minister Manmohan Singh on Thursday asked the states to establish specialized and dedicated forces needed to cripple the "virus". "Although the notions of a red corridor from Nepal to Andhra Pradesh are exaggerated, we have to admit that they have achieved some degree of success in enlarging their areas of mi litancy," Singh said while addressing the Chief Ministers conf erence on internal security. **Indian Express**, December 20, 2007 .

Clearly while India was opening up its economy and entering a faster growth trajectory and while India was even shining, the Naxalites have gathered more momentum. They are now emboldened to frontally take on the Indian state. While they still hold full sway over relatively small areas, they have made an impact in a very large area. They have made the hitherto unconcerned Indian elite, sit up and take notice. The General Secretary of the CPI (Maoist) is no longer coy about boasting about this.[23]

The Enfeebled State

This call to crush Naxalism brings to mind a line from Zafar Gorakhpuri's popular *qawwali* in the form of a competitive duet between Yusuf Azad and Rashida Khatun featured in the 1972 movie Putli Bai. It runs: *"Inke kalai dekho tho chudiyan uthane ke kabhil nahi, phir bhi talwar uthane ki dhamki…"(a look at her wrist tells you that it is not even capable of sustaining the weight of bangles, yet she threatens to lift a sword to strike me down).* I am not alluding to the weight of the PM's *kada*[24] but to the worn out sinews of the State that are now hardly capable of quelling any armed assault upon it, let alone assuaging the causes that force normally compliant people to resort to violence. Having traveled several times through the "Red Corridor" areas in AP, Chhattisgarh, MP and Maharashtra I have little hesitation in testifying that the insurgency has considerable popular support, particularly among the *dalits* and *adivasis* for whom trickle down has meant a little more of little less. In the forested areas of central India, the khaki wearing police, forest and excise departments are truly hated, and this is just about all the government the common people encounter. This is not a mere law and order

[23] **"Q: How much of 'Indian territory' is under Maoist control? The Prime Minister once said 160 out of 604 districts. Was it an exaggeration?**

A: We are indeed flattered by such statistics. But one thing we can understand from the Prime Minister's statement, i.e. how much of a nightmare we have become to the reactionary ruling classes of India. It is an exaggeration to say that Maoists control that many districts, but our influence goes beyond that. " Http://naxalwatch.blogspot.com/2007_09_02_archive.html

[24] A kara or kada or karra is a bangle, worn by both male and femaleinitiated Sikhs. It is one of the five kakars or external articles of faith that identify a Sikh as dedicated to their religious order

problem, but a consequence of a failed state, which could do little to uplift the lives of the tens of millions who inhabit this region. If the state Is serious about rolling back the tide of Naxalism, it needs to undertake nothing less than a total revamp of the system of public administration and adopt new paradigms of equity and justice.

The Government of India has a typically bureaucratic response to this major crisis now gripping the *Adivasi* homelands in six states[25]. The government has already ordered the raising of twenty-five more battalions of armed police, mostly for the CRPF and India Reserve. The Home Minister, P Chidambaram, has launched a somewhat inappropriately named offensive "Operation Greenhunt"[26] to beat down the insurgency. It is indeed unfortunate that the government and the establishment are seeing this as a law and order problem because more coercion by the state will only beget more against it by the aggrieved people.

---

[25] The Red Corridor is a term used to describe an impoverished region in the eastern India that experiences considerable Naxalite activity. These are also areas that suffer from the greatest illiteracy and poverty in modern India, and span parts of AP Bihar, Chhattisgarh, Jharkhand, Karnataka, and MP. Maharashtra, UP and West Bengal. The districts that comprise the Red Corridor are among the poorest in the country. Bihar has the lowest per-capita State Domestic Product of any Indian state, and Uttar Pradesh and Orissa are also among the poorest states in the country. Other areas encompassed by the Red Corridor, such as Chhattisgarh and the Telangana region of Andhra Pradesh, are also either impov-erished or have significant economic inequality, or both. A key characteristic of this region is non-diversified economies that are solely primary sector based. Agriculture, sometimes supplemented with mining or forestry, is the mainstay of the economy, which is often unable to support rapid increases in population.

The areas encompassed by the Red Corridor tend to have stratified societies, with caste and feudal divisions. Several areas also have indigenous tribal populations (or adivasis) who are disadvantaged in their relationship with other components of society. Bihar and Jharkhand have both caste and tribal divisions and violence associated with friction be-tween these social groups. AP's Telangana region similarly has deep caste divides with a relatively strict social hierarchical arrangement. Both Chhattisgarh and Orissa have signifi-cant impoverished tribal populations.

[26] Operation Greenhunt is the name used by the Indian media to describe the Government of India's ongoing paramilitary offensive against the Naxalites. The operation begun in No-vember 2009 along five states in the Red Corridor ."In October 2009, the Central Reserve Police Force (CRPF) announced that it was in the final stages of planning the offensive and had received approval from the government. The Commando Battalion for Resolute Action (COBRA) would take the lead in the operations against Maoist insurgents. At the beginning of November 2009, the first phase of the operation began in Gadichiroli district of Maharashtra state when 18 companies of the CRPF were moved into the area in anticipation of the operation.

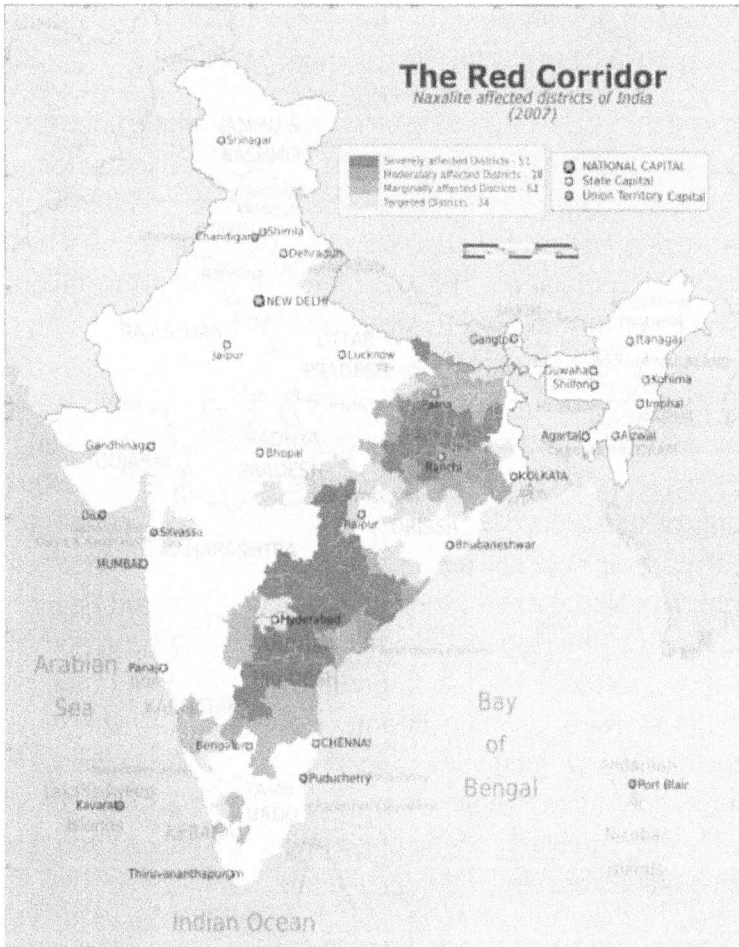

The Red Corridor
Naxalite affected districts of India
(2007)

In his closing remarks in The December 20, 2007 conference, Prime Minister Manmohan Singh said conferences of this nature send a strong message that the "political leadership of the country can rise above our political and party affiliations when it comes to facing national challenges, particularly those concerning internal security." The conference was attended by the full spectrum of national leadership including the BJP and CPM and they all expressed full support for the Prime Minister's rather rare display of determination. It was clear that the entire national leadership was not just speaking but also thinking as one, as if seized by groupthink.

It was the social psychologist Irving Janis[27] who coined the term groupthink to denote faulty decisions a group makes when group pressures and dynamics lead to a deterioration of "mental efficiency, reality testing and moral judgment." In his seminal book Victims of Groupthink[28] published in 1972, Janis analyzed the failures in decision-making that lead to failed outcomes in Pearl Harbor, the Bay of Pigs and the Vietnam War. Janis defined "groupthink" as the tendency of some groups to try to minimize conflict and reach consensus without sufficiently testing, analyzing, and evaluating their ideas. His work showed how pressures for conformity restrict the thinking of the group; bias its analysis, promotes simplistic and stereotyped thinking, and stifles individual creative and independent thought. The Nobel Prize winning scientist Dr. Richard Feynman in his appendix to the Rogers Commission Report of the space shuttle Challenger accident alluded to groupthink prevalent in the higher echelons of NASA, which directly contributed to the disaster. Psychologists now recognize groupthink as a serious disorder and it very simply means that when all are thinking alike nobody is probably really thinking. Signs of it among the nation's top leaders are an ominous portent of things to come.

The Exploitation of the *Adivasis*

The spread of Naxalism is an indication of the sense of desperation and alienation that is sweeping over of large sections of our nation who have been not only systematically marginalized but also cruelly exploited and dispossessed in their last homelands. The late

---

[27] **Irving Lester Janis**   (26 May 1918 - 15 November 1990) was a research psychologist at Yale University and a pr ofessor emeri tus at the University of California at Berkeley most famous for his theory of "groupthink" which described the systematic errors made by groups when taking collective decisions. He retired in 1986.

[28] Janis, Irving (1972). **Victims of Groupthink; A Psychological Study of Foreign-policy Decisions and Fiascoes**   ; Houghton, Mifflin, Boston;   ISBN 978-0395140024.OLC.539682.

Professor Nihar Ranjan Ray[29], one of our most distinguished historians, described the central Indian *adivasis* as "the original autochthonous people of India" meaning that their presence in India pre-dated by far the Dravidians, the Aryans and whoever else settled in this country. The anthropologist Dr. Verrier Elwin[30] states this more emphatically when he wrote: "These are the real swadeshi products of India, in whose presence all others are foreign. These are ancient people with moral rights and claims thousands of years old. They were here first and should come first in our regard." Unfortunately like indigenous people all over the world, the India's *Adivasis* too have been savaged and ravaged by later people claiming to be more "civilized". They still account for almost 8% of India's population and are easily it's most deprived and oppressed section.[31] There are some 573 communities recognized by the government as Scheduled Tribes and therefore eligible to receive special benefits and to compete for reserved seats in legislatures and schools. The biggest tribal group, the Gonds, number about 7.4 million; followed by the Santhals with about 4.2 million. The smallest tribal community is the

---

[29] **Niharranjan Ray** (January 14, 1903 - August 30, 1981) was a historian, well known for his works on history of art and Buddhism. In 1926 he stood first in the M.A. examination in Ancient Indian History and Culture from Calcutta University. He received the *Mrinalini Gold Medal* in the same year for his *Political History of Northern India, AD 600-900* . He was appointed the Chief Librarian in the Central Library of Calcutta University in 1936. He participated in the Quit India movement and was imprisoned from 1943-44. In 1946, he was appointed *Bagishwari Professor of Fine Arts* in Calcutta University and retired from the post in 1965. In 1965, he became the first director of the Indian Institute of Advanced Study, Simla and remained in office till 1970. He was a member of the Third Pay Commission from 1970-73.

[30] **Verrier Elwin** (1902–1964) was a self-trained anthropologist, ethnologist and tribal activist, who began his career in India as a Christian missionary . He was a contr oversial figure who first abandoned the cler gy, to work wi th Gandhiji and the I ndian National Congress, then converted to Hinduism in 1935 after staying a Gandhian ashram, split with the nationalists over what he felt was an overhasty process of transformation and assimilation for the tribal's. Elwin is best known for his early work with the Baigas and Gonds of central India, and he famously married a member of one of the communities he studied there, though he also work on the tribal's of several Northeast Indian states especially in Arunachal Pradesh and settled in Shillong later in life.

[31] **Indigenous peoples** are any ethnic group who inhabit a geographic region with which they have the earliest known historical connection. Several widely accepted formulations, however, which define the term *indigenous peoples* in stricter terms, ha ve been put forward by prominent and internationally recognized organizations, such as the UN, ILO and the World Bank.   contd/-

Chaimal's in the Andaman Islands who number just eighteen. Central India is home to the country's largest tribes, and, taken as a whole, roughly 75 percent of the total tribal population live there.[32]

In the decades after independence the exploitation has only become more rampant. The *adivasi* homelands are rich in natural resources and the new modernizing and industrializing India needs these resources. Today all the mineral resources except oil that India boasts off are to be found only in these areas and the state has not been lax in exploiting them. The only problem is that the people whose homelands were ravaged to extract nature's bounty got little or nothing of it. Even the meager royalties the states receive are mostly expended by the bureaucracy on themselves, as salaries have now become the biggest single expenditure of the Indian states. Sometimes they even exceed all revenues. At last count, before the Sixth Pay Commission's recommendations were implemented, the total wage bill of India's multi-tiered government is a monstrous Rs.193, 000 crores or about 5.6% of the GNP.[33] That the capital expenditure of the central and state governments has come down to about 10% of the annual budgets does not seem to worry the eminent economist who presides over the Planning Commission.

Other related terms for indigenous peoples include   aborigines, aboriginal people, native people, first people, and autochthonous. "Indigenous peoples" may often be used in preference to these or other terms as a neutral replacement, where such terms may have taken on negative or pejorative connotations by their prior association and use. It is the preferred term in use by the United Nations and its subsidiary organizations. In Indian officialese they are referred to as Scheduled Tribes or ST's.

Scheduled Tribe members represented only 8 percent of the total population (about 68 million). They were found in 1991 in the greatest numbers in Orissa (7 million, or 23 percent of the state's population), Maharashtra (7.3 million, or 9 per cent), and Madhya Pradesh (15.3 million, or 23 per cent). In proportion, however, the populations of states in the northeast had the greatest concentrations of Scheduled Tribe members. For example, 31 percent of the population of Tripura, 34 percent of Manipur, 64 per cent of Arunachal Pradesh, 86 percent of Meghalaya, 88 percent of Nagaland, and 95 percent of Mizoram were Scheduled Tribe members. Other heavy concentrations were found in Dadra and Nagar Haveli, 79 per cent of which was composed of Scheduled Tribe members, and Lakshadweep, with 94 percent of its population being Scheduled Tribe members.

[32] Http://tribal.nic.in/indiamap.html - State wise Tribal Population percentage in India.

[33] **The Planning Commission** does not foresee any significant disruption of state finances on account of increase in salaries of state government employees. "I don't think that this disruption is going to be all that crucial," Commission Deputy Chairman Montek Singh

We all now know very well that big government in the absence of a responsive nervous system actually means little government, and whatever little interaction the people at the bottom have with the state is usually a none too happy one. In the vast Central Indian highlands the occasional visit of an official invariably means extraction by coercion of what little the poor people have. It doesn't just end with a chicken or a goat or a bottle of *mahua*[34], it often includes all these and the modesties of the womenfolk. Most tribal villages and settlements have no access to schools and medical care. Very few are connected with all weather roads. Perish the thought of electricity though all the coal and most of the hydel projects to generate electricity are in the tribal regions. The forests have been pillaged and the virgin forests thick with giant teak and sal trees are things of the past.

In Orissa over 72% of all *adivasis* live well below the poverty line.[35] At the national level 45.86% of all *adivasis* live below the

Ahluwalia said on the possible impact of adoption of the Sixth Pay Commission award by the state governments. The Pay Commission, constituted by the Centre, is expected to submit its report by early April and the state governments would be under pressure to revise the salary of state employees, once that happens. Pointing out that blind adoption of the Pay Commission award by the state governments is not a good idea, Ahluwalia said pay commissions are constituted once in 10 years and the states can do many things to neutralize the impact. The government, he said, was made to effect a big increase in salaries of its employees at the end of 10 years as the dearness allowance (DA) does not adequately take care of inflation. "So at the end of 10 years, the government will be benefiting from a squeeze in real pay because the DA was never enough so you have a big increase," he added.

[34] *Madhuca longifolia*, commonly known as **mahwa** or **mahua**, is a tropical tree found largely in the central and north Indian plains and forests. It is a fast growing tree that grows to approximately 20 meters in height, possesses evergreen or semi-evergreen foliage, and belongs to the family Sapotaceae. It is adapted to arid environments, being a prominent tree in tropical mixed deciduous forests in India in the states of Jharkhand, Uttar Pradesh, Bihar, Madhya Pradesh, Kerala, Gujarat and Orissa. The flowers are used to produce an alcoholic drink in tropical India. Several parts of the tree, including the bark, are used for their medicinal properties. It is considered holy by many tribal communities because of its usefulness. The tree is considered a boon by the tribal's who are forest dwellers and they are keen conservators of this tree. However, the conservation of the tree has been marginalized as it is stated that the non-tribal's do not favor propagation of this tree. [

[35] **Adivasis of South Orissa: Enduring Poverty** . Sanjay Kumar. *Economic and Political Weekly*, Vol. 36, No. 43 (Oct. 27 - Nov. 2, 2001), pp. 4052-4054. (article consists of 3 pages)

poverty line. Incidentally the official Indian poverty line is a nothing more than a starvation line,[36] which means that almost half of India's original inhabitants go to bed every night starving. Several anthropometric studies have revealed that successive generations of *adivasis* are actually becoming smaller unlike all other people in India who benefit from better and increasingly nutritious diets. What little the Indian state apportions to the welfare and development of indigenous people gets absorbed in the porous layers of our government. The late Rajiv Gandhi once famously said that less than 15% of the money allocated to rural areas actually percolated down.[37]

A typical instance of this is in the eight tribal majority KBK (Kalahandi, Bolangir and Koraput)[38] districts of Orissa where over Rs.2000 crores cumulatively spent ostensibly on social welfare and rural development schemes during the past three years has just vanished leaving little or no evidence of doing any good to the intended recipients. The people are not having any more of it and have taken to coercing the state, dishing out to it what its minions have been doing for ages.

---

[36] For a detailed discussion see " **Redefining Poverty: A New Poverty Line for a New India**" by Mohan Guruswamy and Ronald Abraham, Centre for Policy Alternatives. www.cpasindia.org

[37] **Times of India** of 14 October 2009: "Twenty-five years after Rajiv Gandhi said that for every rupee sent to the common man, only 17 paise reached him, the debate is back on what constitutes a huge indictment of the delivery system in welfare schemes.   Prime Minister Manmohan Singh told reporters in Mumbai on Sunday that leakage of funds was not as big as mentioned by Rajiv Gandhi. "Leakage of funds earmarked for development does exist but I don't admit these leakages are as big as was mentioned by   Rajivji," he said.

By coincidence, a day later, Planning Commission deputy chairman Montek Singh Ahluwalia told a seminar that the former PM was correct about the extent of leakage. He said a Plan panel study on PDS recently found that only 16 paise out of a rupee was reaching the targeted poor; as he went on to suggest that 1% of every scheme money be earmarked for monitoring and evaluation.

While their opinion on the magnitude of pilferage may differ, the top policy duo has cranked open a debate at the core of the campaign f   or 'aam aadmi'. When Rajiv Gandhi spoke during a visit to Kalahandi in 1985, it was an indictment of the system in the pre-reforms era, which trigger ed a controv ersy. "

[38] The KBK districts account for 19.80% population over 30.60% geographical area of the State. 89.95% people of this region still live in villages. Lower population density (153

The migration of non-tribals is a long story. Way back in 1945 the Revenue Department of the Nizam's Government in Hyderabad commissioned the Austrian anthropologist, Christoph von Furer-Haimendorf,[39] to study the condition of tribals in the state and make appropriate policy recommendations.[40] The four studies of the tribal groups in the northern areas of Hyderabad narrate how in the settled villages of the tribal areas, outsiders owned most of the land under cultivation. A typical instance is the Koya (Gond) village of Ragleyanguda in Yellandu taluq. The total area under cultivation here was 1616 acres. Of a Koya population of 254, there were only five Koya *pattadars* who together owned 24 acres in all. It is the same story today and the Adivasi has been pushed further into the remaining jungle or into menial existence while the land has been

---

persons / sq.km) in comparison to 236 for Orissa indicates difficult living conditions and an undeveloped economy. Tribal communities dominate this region. As per 2001 Census, about 38.41% people of these districts belong to the Scheduled T ribes (ST) communities including four primitive tribal groups (PTG), i.e., Bondas, Dadai, Langia Sauas and Dangaria Kandhas. In addition, 16.25% population belongs to the Scheduled Castes (SC) communities. Literacy rates are also far below the State as well as National averages.   Female literacy is only 29.10%. As per the 1997 census of BPL families, about 71% families in the region live below the poverty line.

[39] Christoph Von Fure r-Haimendorf was born on June 22, 1909 in Vienna, Austria. When Christoph was young, he dreamt of going to India to see what it was like to live there. He felt that the best way to travel to India would be to experience it as an Anthropologist. To make Christoph's dream come true, he went to the University of Vienna and worked hard to build a career as an Anthropologist. There he studied archaeology and physical anthropology and acquired his doctorate in anthropology by writing his thesis on a comparison of two peoples in the northeast area of India.

World War 2 broke out when Christoph tried again to return to India. As a native of Germany with a German passport, he was arrested. To his luck though, he was relocated to study other groups of people that weren't very well studied or understood at all. These different groups, the Chenchu's and the Reddi's interested him because he was able to compare the peoples he was studying now to the Naga Hill people he had previously studied. After the w ar w as o ver, he w as appointed to be the Advisor f or T ribes and Backward Classes to Nizam's Government of Hyderabad and helped to deal with the new issue of land reform of the peoples. Christoph's goal was to make sure that modernization did not phase out the culture and language of the people, which he w as in charge of. In 1949, he was given a lectureship at School of Oriental and African Studies. From there his educational work really sky rocketed. In 2 years, he went from a lectur er to reader, then Chair of Asian Anthropology. The following 25 years he was there, he encouraged the use of fieldwork to enrich studies for both student and faculty alike.

[40] **Tribal Hyderabad – Four Reports** by Christoph von Furer-Haimendorf published by the Revenue Department, Government of H.E.H the Nizam, Hyderabad 1945.

appropriated by Hindu and Muslim settlers. They are now the majority in only a fraction of their original homelands.

The Land of the Koitur

There is a vast and mostly forested region spanning almost the entire midriff of India from Orissa to Gujarat, lying between the westbound Narmada and eastbound Godavari, bounded by many mountain ranges like the Vindhya, Satpura, Mahadeo, Meykul, and Abujhmar, that was once the main home of the original autochthonous Indian, the *Adivasi*. Though this is the home of many tribal groups, the largest tribal group, the Gonds, dominated the region. The earliest Gond kingdom appears to date from the 10th century and the Gond Rajas were able to maintain a relatively independent existence until the 18th century, although they were compelled to offer nominal allegiance to the Mughal Empire. The great historian Jadunath Sarkar records: "In the sixteenth and seventeenth century much of the modern Central Provinces (today's MP) were under the sway of aboriginal Gond chiefs and was known under the name of Gondwana. A Mughal invasion and the sack of the capital had crippled the great Gond kingdom of Garh-Mandla in Akbar's reign and later by Bundela encroachments from the north. But in the middle of the seventeenth century another Gond kingdom with its capital at Deogarh, rose to greatness, and extended its sway over the districts of Betul, Chindwara, and Nagpur, and portions of Seoni, Bhandara and Balaghat. In the southern part of Gondwana stood the town of Chanda, the seat of the third Gond dynasty and hereditary foe and rival of the Raja of Deogarh." But the glory of Deogarh departed when the Maratha ruler of Nagpur annexed Deogarh after the death of Chand Sultan.[41] Incidentally the Gond ruler of Deogarh, Bakht Buland, founded the city of Nagpur. Jadunath Sarkar writes about him thus: "He lived to extend the area, power and prosperity of his kingdom very largely and to give the greatest trouble to Aurangzeb

---

[41] " pp 338 -344 f rom "**A Short History of Aurangazib** " by Jadunath Sarkar, Orient Blackswan ISBN 978-81-250-3690-6

in the last years of his reign." In fact the one big reason Aurangzeb could not deploy all his power against Shivaji, was because the Gond kings were constantly at war with the Mughals and kept interdicting the lines from the Deccan to Agra. But of course the history of modern India is not generous to them.

Jabalpur was another one of the major centers of the Garh-Mandla kingdom and like other major dynastic capitals had a large fort and palace. Temples and palaces with extremely fine carvings and erotic sculptures came up throughout the Gond kingdoms. The temple of Bhoramdeo at Kawardha[42] in Chhattisgarh still stands as a testimony to levels of culture and craft attained during the heydays of the Gonds.

During the British days this region constituted much of the Central Provinces of India later to become Madhya Pradesh. This is the main home of about seven million Gond people who are India's largest single tribal grouping.[43] The Gonds are now a culturally and linguistically heterogeneous people having attained much cultural uniformity with the dominant linguistic influences of their region. Thus, the Gonds of the eastern and northwestern Madhya Pradesh region that now includes the new state of Chattisgarh speak Chattisgarhi and western Hindi. But the Gonds of Bastar, which is at the southeastern end of this vast region and a part of Chattisgarh, are

---

[42] The **Bhoramdeo Temple** Set amidst the picturesque surroundings of Maikal Mountains and dense forests near Kawardha (134 kms from Raipur) is a perfect blend of religious and erotic sculptures. It is carved on the rocky stones in the Nagar style. This temple was built in the period of 7th to 11th century A.D.   The Shiva Lingam in the temple is beautifully carved and the artistic appeal beckons the visitors. The Bhoramdeo temple has a resemblance with the Sun temple of Konark and the Khajuraho temples , and that is why it is also called the Khajuraho of Chhattisgarh. The "Madwa Mahal" near the Bhoramdeo temple is another beautiful historic monument, worth seeing. Madwa Mahal is known as the memorial of the marriage of Nagwanshi king and Haihawanshi Queen. 'Madwa' is a word from the local dialect synonymous to marriage pandal

[43] Anthropometric and Genetic distance between Gonds of Central India; by Urmila Pingle in American Journal of Physical Anthr opology. 1984 Nov; 65(3): 291-304 A morphological and genetic study was undertaken on five Gondi-speaking populations of Central India (Andhra Pradesh and Maharashtra States). There has been no systematic biological study on this large Dravidian-speaking tribal group, amounting to 13% of the total tribal population of India. Data was collected on 16 anthropometric measurements and seven genetic markers (blood groups, hemoglobin, G6PD and plasma protein polymorphisms) on the Raj

different in this respect. Though there are many tribal groups like the Halbas, Bhatras, Parjas and Dorlas, the Maria and Bison Horned Gonds are the most numerous. The language spoken by them, like that of the Koyas of AP is an intermediate Dravidian language closer to Telugu and Kanarese. There is a history to this.

According to Sir WV Grigson, ICS. who in 1938 wrote the still widely referred to "The Maria Gonds of Bastar"[44], the Bastar princely family was descended from the Kakatiya kings who reigned at Warangal from AD 1150 to 1425. According to Bastar tradition and folk songs after Pratap Rudra Raya, the greatest of the Kakatiya kings was killed in battle with the invading forces of Ahmad Shah Bahmani, his brother Annam Deo fled across the Godavari into Bastar. Bastar was then constituted of a group of loosely held feudal dependencies of Warangal.

Annam Deo then founded a line that continued till 1966 when the last ruler, the much revered Pravir Chandra Bhanj Deo was killed at the instance of the MP government of Dwarka Prasad Mishra for having resisted the Congress party's attempts to extend its influence into the region and for championing the rights of the tribal people.

Gonds, Kolams, Manne, Koyas and Plains Maria Gonds. Various genetic distance measures such as Mahalanobis's D2 and Nei's and Sanghvi's measures and cluster analysis techniques were used to determine the relationship between these groups based on anthropometrics and genetic variables. The statistical analysis revealed the Gonds to be a heterogeneous group in both morphology and genetic characteristics. The morphological and genetic distances between these five groups when projected graphically revealed that the spatial distribution of these Gonds generally corresponds to their present geographical distribution. However, the actual relationships between each of the Gond populations show differences when based on these two biological variables, the possible reasons for this being discussed in the paper. The emphasis of this study is on the importance of geographical proximity in producing morphological and genetic similarity between populations, brought about by a short distance as well as similar geographical factors (such as soil, terrain, flora, etc.) drawing these populations together under a common ecocul tural umbrella.

[44] **Sir Wilfred Grigson's** detailed, accurate, and comprehensive ethnographic study, **Maria Gonds of Bastar**, first publ ished in 1938, has at tained the status of a classic of Indian tribal studies. This is a reprint of the 1949 reissue with commentary and a forty-page note by the author on the Maria Gonds of Chanda and Durg.   Publisher: Oxford University Press, USA; 2nd Impression. Edition (March 12, 1992) ISBN-100195628551 ISBN-13: 978-0195628555

When Pravir Chandra ascended the *gadi* in 1936 he was the twentieth in his line to reign in Bastar. Such is the reverence for Pravir Chandra Bhanj Deo among the tribal's that even today his pictures are sold in the shops at the entrance of the great Danteshwari temple at Dantewara.[45]

Telugu inscriptions at the temple town of Barsur and Kuruspal on the Indrawati River tell of a line of Telugu kings, the Nagavansi that ruled Bastar even as early as the eleventh century. But this is not important anymore. What is relevant is that the Gonds of Bastar are now considered by anthropologists to be a distinct group and are referred to as the "Koitur". Grigson even writes that the Maria and Bison Horned Gonds of Bastar resent being called Gonds.

Wherever the Gonds still speak their own language they refer to themselves as *Koi* or *Koitur*. It is only in the Telugu regions that a name close to what they call themselves, *Koya*, is used for them. Anthropologists generally refer to only these "Teluguized" Gonds as Koitur and even though there are large groups of Koitur living in AP and Maharashtra, Bastar is truly the land of the Koitur. The old Bastar state when it was incorporated into independent India as a district of the former Central Provinces was an area as large as the state of Kerala.[46] This district has been made into two with a second district Dantewara carved out of it, and with the old Antagarh tehsil now becoming a part of Kanker district.

---

[45] Pravir Chandra Bhanj Deo 25 June 1929 - 25 March 1966 was the 20th Maharaja of Bastar who was killed in 1966 by the then Congressgovernment of Madhya Pradesh for championing the cause of his subjects. He fought for rights of the tribal people. His subjects adored the last K akatiya ruler of B astar. He was born in 25 June 1929 and wa s educated at R ajkumar College, Raipur. He suc ceeded to throne on 28 October 1936.

He was immensely popular among his people, as he took up the cause of the local tribal's, and provided political leadership against exploitation of natural resources of the region, and corruption in land reforms, thus he was perceived a threat by the then ruling congress people. On March 25, 1966 he was killed in police firing at the steps of his own palace at Jagdalpur along with many of the royal court. Officially the death toll was twelve including the ex-king and wounded were twenty; the police had fired sixty-one rounds.

[46] Bastar state was situated in the south-eastern corner of the former Central Provinces and Berar, bounded north by the Kanker State, south b y the Godav ari district of the Agency area of the Madras Presidency , west b y Chanda district of the f ormer princely state of

I have been visiting Bastar since I was a teenager in the mid 1960's when I crossed the Godavari with my father in pursuit of a man-eating leopard near the village of Pujari Kanker nestled in the Abalaka range. Since then a great many changes have come about, as they have elsewhere, and have mostly been to the disadvantage of the Adivasi. The process of Hinduization combined with Hindi culture has reduced the egalitarian Koitur to the bottom of the social strata. Dr. Kalyan Kumar Chakravarthy, Director of the Indira Gandhi Rashtriya Manav Sangrahalaya, Bhopal has written eloquently and cogently on this in his concluding chapter "Extinction or Adaptation of the Gonds" in the book "Tribal Identity in India" also edited by him.[47] The Sangrahalaya established for the exclusive study, research and preservation for posterity the unique aspects of India's tribal societies and their culture, has most beautifully and imaginatively recreated these on the Shamla Hills overlooking Bhopal's magnificent lake. Public attitudes in metropolitan India however seem to have been conditioned by the works of artists like JP Singhal[48] who has through his popular calendar art of bare breasted tribal women titillated millions and served to establish the generally prevalent view of these people. Popular Indian cinema has consistently depicted tribals in a lurid and garish manner. It is common to have them painted black and dancing in grass skirts in a new musical genre called the Bollywood Tribal Fusion.[49] Even the

---

Hyderabad, and the Godavari river, and east by the Jeypore estate in Orissa. It had an area of 13,062 square miles (33,830 km²). **Kerala** is a state in southwestern India. It was created on 1 November 1956, with the passing of the States Reorganization Act bringing together the areas where Malayalam is the dominant language. The state has an area of 38,863 kms².

[47] **Tribal identity in India: Extinction or Adaptation!** Published in 1996, Indira Gandhi Rashtriya Manav Sangrahalaya Bhopal, India). LCCN 97906674; Dewey: 305.8.00954; LC: GN635.I4 T6743 1996.

[48] A legendary name in calendar art, J P Singhal is best known as the man who popularized calendar painting as an art form. For a period of 35 years he ruled the world of calendar design producing over 2500 paintings on a v ariety of subjects including mythology , children, tribals and rural India. With over 75 crore reproductions of his paintings, Singhal was singularly responsible for popularizing art in households.   http://www.indiaprwire.com/pressrelease/art/2010022344138.htm

[49] You'll see it done with tribals too. Hae you noticed how Bollywood portrays its "tribals" with a distinctly (stereotypical) African flavor? The most famous example, of course, is that

Ramayana cannot be deemed exempt of having nurtured certain attitudes about *Adivasis.* What was the monkey army about? If we have to give it the status of a historical narrative then are we to believe that talking monkeys existed? Or possibly a now extinct race of androids? Or was it poetic license that the writers took to describe indigenous people in the manner they were thought of? More likely is that it reflected prevalent racial attitudes at the time of writing that persist because of the sanctified status of the mythology.[50] Several scholars have indeed written about this, but the need to be politically correct is overridden by popular belief and sentiment.

Much of the dense forests of Bastar have since been chopped down and the animals hunted to near extinction. Once great herds of wild buffalo have been reduced to a mere handful precariously surviving near Kutru. There are only a few tigers left in the beautiful Kanger Valley Reserve.[51] The traditional existence of the Koitur is as much threatened. Migrants from other parts, now increasingly from the Hindi speaking areas of old Madhya Pradesh have settled in large numbers and have reduced the indigenous population to a

---

weird group of "tribals" , people in blackface no less, marching through the forest in the middle of the night in **Shalimar** chanting "*Oo la la la hoo, Oo la la la hoo, phurr phurr* ", while Dharmendra sings, " *Hum bewafa hargiz na the ...*" http://indiequill.wordpress.com/2007/06/20/indias-gypsy-rom-elsewhere/

[50] In **The Aryan Debate** / ed. by Thomas R. T rautmann. - New Delhi : Oxf ord University Press. 2005. - xliv, 289 S. ll., Kt. - (Oxford in India Readings : Debates in Indian History and Society). ISBN 0-19-566908-8, Trautman writes that the Ramayana is a story of conflict between the Aryans and the indigenous people of the 'Indian' land. This viewpoint has been accepted by many historians. The description of Rama as a tall, fair, sharp nosed etc shows uncanny resemblance to the 'Vedic people' or the Aryans, the stock of people who migrated from central Asia and settled in the Indian subcontinent. When they first inter-acted with the 'locals', they gained a superiorit y complex due to their looks, li festyle and their warring style. Their superiority complex is visible by   the way they describe the indigenous people, for example Ravana is described as dark, snub nosed, squat, muscular and hairy . He is also depicted as a worshipper   of cults that hav e tribal ingredients. The descriptions match the Dravidian stalk of indigenous people. The animal army of Rama can be easily interpreted as the   people of different tribes, whose names were those of animals, like the tribe of langur, the tribe of bears. Even if this point is prone to debates, it cannot be denied that all   the tribes even today contain these totems.

[51] For a better understanding of the richness of fauna in these regions read " **Wild animals in Central India**" by A.A.Dunbar Brander, Natraj Publishers, Dehra Dun, ISBN: 81-8158-117-4

minority in many areas particularly in and around Jagdalpur and Kondagaon.

The National Mineral Development Corporation, a PSU, operates India's largest iron ore mine in Bailadilla in Dantewara district.[52] Instead of bringing prosperity to the local people it has done irrevocable harm. Few benefits of this economic exploitation have trickled down to them while the ecological degradation of the area is devastating. Even worse has been the social degradation that has visited the Koitur Gonds in general and the sexual exploitation of their women in particular by people from the so-called civilized sections and regions of India.[53]

Enter the Telugu Speakers

The migration of Telugu speaking people in the areas near the Godavari has also continued unabated and they have done in southern Bastar what they have done in Adilabad, Warangal, Khammam and East Godavari. They have swamped the tribal population, exploited them mercilessly and have reduced them to penury and second class citizenship in their ancient lands. And quite ironically it is from these that the nucleus of the Naxalite leadership has emerged. Though the Naxal movement is now almost entirely centered in the *Adivasi* homelands, one cannot but notice a disconnect between what the tribals seek and what the Naxalites provide. Few adivasis have heard of Mao Zedong or care for what he stood and did. The Naxalites on the other hand deify him. To them that China's Chairman is still the Chairman! They are steeped in the dialectics and folklore of that phase of China. Few of them have

---

[52] Incorporated in 1958 as Government of India, fully owned public enterprise. **NMDC** is under the administrative control of the Ministry of Steel, Government of India. Since inception involved in the exploration of wide range of minerals including iron ore, copper, rock phosphate, lime stone, dolomite, gypsum, bentonite, magnesite, diamond, tin, tungsten, graphite, beach sands etc. India's single largest iron ore producer and exporter, presently producing about 30 million tons of iron ore from 3 fully mechanized mines viz., Bailadila Deposit-14/11C, Bailadila Deposit-5, 10/11A (Chhattisgarh State) and Donimalai Iron Ore Mines (Karnataka State) which are awarded ISO 9001-2000 certification.

[53] pp 88, Chapter, **"Development and the Future of Tribals** " by Indra Deva in "Social Science and Social Concern" Ed. By S.B. Chakrabarti. Mittal Publications, Delhi 110035, ISBN 81-7099-062-9

studied Mao or have even read about him. One even doubts if any of the St. Stephens or Presidency College students who so romanticized Mao would have known much about him.[54]

I recall a rather surreal conversation I had with a group of Andhra University students who had taken to the hills with the PWG. In late 1983, I was on my way to Chintur in East Godavari district and was driving down from Bhadrachallam skirting the Bastar border. At the village of Edugurallapalle (literally means seven horse village possibly because it was an official horse station with provision to stable seven horses in the old Asaf Jahi days?), my companion and I ran into some Naxal's. Like college educated young people they were quite eager to get into a discussion and soon the discussion veered around to the internecine battle between the various groups. My new friends described one of the other major factions as Lin Piaoist[55] and

---

[54] **"The Private Life of Chairman Mao** " by his long time personal physician Dr. Zhisui Li. (Random House 1996, ISBN-10: 0679764437) According to the book, Li witnessed Mao's private life on a day-to-day basis, mostly dealing with Mao at the height of his powers. Li alleged that Mao appeared anxious of the public but was indifferent to the problems of the Chinese people. It also describes Mao's signs of illness, paranoia, as well as neglecting dental hygiene (Mao's teeth were coated with a green-colored film, and when Li touched Mao's gums, pus oozed out). The book details Mao's alleged personal depravity and sexual politics. It is also an account of the political intrigue within   Communist Party leadership, excessive use of propaganda (such as putting rice fields near railroad tracks), as well as Mao's excitement after Richard Nixon's visit to China, around the time his health started to deteriorate.

Mao most admired the Emperor Qin Shihuangdi (reign 221-206 BC) who founded Imperial China. Qin vastly expanded China by absorbing small nations. He constructed roads and canals, introduced weights and measures and began building the Great Wall. Qin also killed and persecuted wantonly . He kil led Confucian scholars and burned classical books. Bu t Mao considered all these minor aberrations and argued that the good outweighed the bad. This was Mao's attitude when he was told that over 10 million people died in the 159-61 famines after the Peoples Communes were formed. Just like Bal Thackeray's admiration for Adolf Hitler because he built autobahns and Germany powerful!

[55] **Lin Biao** , born as Lin Yurong; (December 5, 1907– September 13, 1971) w as a Chinese communist military leader who was instrumental in the communist victory in the Chinese Civil War, especially in Northeastern China, and w as the General who led the Peoples Liberation Army into Beijing in 1949. He abstained from becoming a major player in politics until he rose to prominence during the Cultural Revolution, climbing as high as second-in-charge and Mao Zedong's designated and constitutional successor and comrade-in-arms.

He died in a 'plane crash' in September 1971 in   Mongolia after what appeared to be a failed coup to oust Mao. After his death, he was officially condemned as a traitor, and is still recognized as one of the two "major Counter-revolutionary parties" during the Cultural Revolution– the other being Mao's last wife Jiang Qing– for which he is assigned a large portion of blame.

considered them the main enemy of their faction.[56] Like amoeba the CPI (ML) founded by Charu Mazumdar has undergone frequent meiosis and mitosis, splitting and uniting all the time. If it didn't have so many bloody consequences it might even be quite funny. At last count there are no less than fifteen Naxalite parties. The sheer absurdity of sitting in the jungles of Dandakaranya and debating the merits or otherwise of the departed Lin Biao did not seem to strike them at all. What had all this got to do with the immediate problems of the *adivasi* people?

Yet today the entire greater homeland of the Koitur Gonds in Maharashtra, Chattisgarh and Andhra Pradesh is under the thrall of the Telugu speaking Naxalite leadership, which now has an increasingly symbiotic relationship with rapacious forest and PWD contractors, and corrupt officialdom. But it is in remote and isolated Bastar that the insurgency has found a true home and has had its greatest impact. Yet this is not an isolated insurgency as the Telangana insurgency of the late 1940's was.[57] The forest tracts of the central Indian highlands are almost contiguous and link up with the forests of Chota Nagpur in Jharkhand and are easily linked with the Nepali Terai where a fraternal party is now a major player in working out new constitutional arrangements. Its thirty thousand combatants sit in UN maintained camps as the political process goes on.

---

[56] The pro-Charu Mazumdar CPI (ML) later split into pro and anti-Lin Biao factions. The pro-Lin Biao group NBBRC became known as Central Organizing Committee / Communist Party of India (Marxist–Leninist) (Shanti Pal) and the anti-Lin Biao-group later became known as Communist Party of India (Marxist-Leninist) Liberation.

[57] **The Telangana Rebellion** was a Communist led peasant revolt that took place in the former princely state of Hyderabad   between 1946 and 1951. The Communist Party of India led this revolt. The revolt began in the   Nalgonda district and quickly spread to the Warangal and Bidar districts. Peasant farmers and labourers revolted against the Nizam and the local feudal landlords (jagirdars and deshmukhs)) who were loyal to the Nizam. The initial modest aims were to do away with the illegal and excessive exploitation meted out by these f eudal lor ds in the name of bonded labour. The most strident demand was for the writing off of all debts of the peasants that were manipulated by the feudal lords.

At the same time the Nizam was resisting the Indian government's efforts to bring Hyderabad into the new Indian union. The government sent the army in September 1948 to incorporate Hyderabad into Indian Union. The Communist party instigated the peasants

Enemies of the Brahmin Samaj!

During my last visit to Bastar a few years ago, I encountered well-armed insurgent groups in two different places. On my way from Narainpur to Barsur on the forest road along the base of the Abujhumar Mountains, we ran into a roadblock laid by visibly armed men just a few kilometers out of Chota Dongar. Providentially it was on a straight road and I was able to stop my vehicle at some distance and reverse my direction of travel. Back at Chota Dongar where a large weekly market was underway as we stopped to catch our breath and also to witness the cockfights, we ran into a bunch of very scared, very drunk, and very armed policemen who insisted we see photographs of what a Naxalite squad had done to a colleague the week before on the same road. His head was smashed with boulders. When we told them of our encounter with the other side just a short distance down the road, they showed absolutely no interest in engaging them and strongly urged us to return to Narainpur, which we promptly did.

The forest bungalow at Narainpur is right opposite the main bus stand and when we went out that evening to make calls to our homes, the phone booth owner told us about what happened just a short while earlier. It seems that a group of armed policemen had boarded a bus bound from Chota Dongar for Narainpur. Midway, near Mahimagawadi, the bus was stopped and a group of armed Naxalites boarded it. The policemen were at the rear of the bus and the Naxalites sat in the front. In between sat many terrified passengers. The bus made its way to its destination and all aboard, the enemies

---

to use guerilla tactics and around 3000 villages (about 41000 sq. kilometers) came under peasant-rule. The landlords were either killed or driven out and the land was redistributed. These victorious villages established communes reminiscent of Sovlet Mlr (socials) to administer their region. These community governments were integrated regionally into a central organization. The CPI under the banner of Andhra Mahasabha led the rebellion . Few among the well-known individuals at the forefront of the movement were great leaders like P. Sundarayya, M. Basavapunniah, C. Rajeshwara Rao, Raavi Narayana Reddy, the Urdu poet Makhdoom Mohiuddin, Hassan Nasir, Arutla Ramachandra Reddy and his wife Kamala Bai and others. Sundarayya became the Gen. Secretary of the CPM and Rajeshwara Rao of the CPI after the split in 1964.

of the state, the agents of the inimical state and innocent villagers alike disembarked and dispersed into the night. Quite clearly there is a balance of terror now in Bastar that forces co-existence. The gun ruled and the state has almost entirely withered away.

After the formation of Chattisgarh political power, instead of reflecting the tribal density and aspirations, generally passed into the hands of the Hindu elite. For a short period the new state had in Ajit Jogi, a former IAS officer and professedly a tribal belonging to the Marwahi tribe, as its first Chief Minister. Jogi was controversial from the very beginning. His tribal status was challenged in the courts. He was also a Christian. He faced many corruption charges, but this degree of corruption is just par for the course for an Indian politician. Nevertheless the ire of the Hindu upper castes are reserved for the dalits and adivasis who grab office from the traditional groups who provide the leadership to all of India's major political parties. Perhaps the biggest recommendation for him came from a Sub-inspector of Police in Narayanpur who fired a flaming glob of spittle reddened by *paan* at an invisible Ajit Jogi and described him as an enemy of the Brahmin Samaj. To be that in Bastar, where the real enemy is the creeping Hinduization with all its attendant values and exclusionary practices, seems to me a good start to the process of saving its tribal society from extinction. All over the rest of India's central highlands our policies by forcing the Adivasis to merge their identities with that of the encroaching culture have crushed them into a becoming a feeble and self-pitying underclass.

The armed police first went into Bastar, now in Chhattisgarh in 1966. The Gond people in Bastar revolted against the corrupt and exploitative ways of the Madhya Pradesh Congress government of DP Mishra. Pandit DP Mishra, a Sanskrit scholar of some repute, was very closely identified with the powerful *bidi* and *tendu* leaf interests in Madhya Pradesh. He was also a Hindu traditionalist with all the social habits and prejudices of the Brahmin orthodoxy. His interest in Bastar was mainly for its abundance of tendu leaves and teak in its rich forests. In those days the Bastar forest began at Keskal and went down all the way to the Godavari in the south, and the Sabari in the east. Even today you can see remnants of the virgin teak forests in Abujhumar that will give you an idea of what this forest was like. All that has now long vanished. The forests have receded south of Jagdalpur and even around Dantewara, what you see are leftovers of that great forest.

DP Mishra's government began the vandalization of Bastar that continues even today. When the *adivasis* began to protest against this assault on their habitat and began rallying around the traditional ruler, Mishra unleashed the police. Matters came to a head on 25 March 1966 when the police fired on the *adivasi's* who congregated in Jagdalpur to pay the customary Dussera homage to their Raja, Pravir Chandra Bhanj Deo. Not only did the MP police kill scores of *adivasis*, but they also gunned down the Raja in his home in cold blood. Soon after this incident central forces were deployed in Bastar and one got a first hand look at the havoc they wrought. The armed forces only repeated what they had done in the Naga Hills. In those days the armed forces used Lee Enfield .303 rifles and the adivasis used bows and arrows and the occasional muzzle-loading gun. With the advent of the AK-47 capable of delivering over 650 rounds per minute combined with an intimate knowledge of the terrain, the Naxalites, now mostly *adivasi* volunteers are not as disadvantaged as before. In the recent months the police have been at the receiving end and the Prime Minister is a worried man.

The only sign of the state here were the pockmarked buildings that once housed government schools and primary health centers (PHC's). At the village *haat* near Dantewara, as we stood watching cockfights a naxal patrol quietly came along and took *talashi* of our vehicle. They had a few good laughs over the cartons of mineral water we were carrying but refused to pose for pictures. Two days prior to this the vehicle was stopped and searched in AP's Warangal district by an armed police patrol. The Sub-inspector leading the team was drunk, as were most of his men. The first question was whether we were carrying firearms? Then they wanted to know how much cash we were carrying? Then things got a bit hairy. They wanted to know as to how we had entered the forest area without "permission". One got the distinct feeling that only our facility with English and the Delhi license plates prevented an encounter. And now Dr. Manmohan Singh's only serious proposal is to raise twenty-five more battalions of such fine fighting men to defend our democratic way of life and to uphold the Constitution?

Clearly there are two distinct reasons for the present unrest in the *Adivasi* homelands of India. The first and probably the more important one is the struggle for identity against the creeping Hinduization or de-culturisation of *Adivasi* society. *Adivasi* society was built on a foundation of equality. People were given respect and status according to their contribution to social needs but only while they were performing that particular function. Such a value-system was sustainable as long as the *Adivasi* community was non-acquisitive and all the products of society were shared. Adivasi society has been under constant pressure as the money economy grew and made traditional forms of barter less difficult to sustain.[58]

In his well-regarded ethnographic monograph "The Reddi's of Bison Hills", the anthropologist Christoph von Furer-Haimendorf[59]

---

[58] "In mat ters of tr ade, the **Adivasis** followed a highly ev olved system of honour . All agreements that they entered into were honoured, often the entire tribe chipping in to honor an agreement made by an individual member of the tribe. Individual dishonesty or deceit was punished severely by the tribe. An individual who acted in a manner that violated the honor of the tribe faced potential banishment and family members lost the right to participate in community events during the period of punishment. But often, tribal integrity was undermined because the non-tribal's who traded with the Adivasis reneged on their promises and took advantage of the sincerity and honesty of most members of the tribe." ht tp://india_resource.tripod.com/adivasi.html

[59] At the end of the war, **Haimendorf** was appointed to the position of **Advisor for Tribes and Backward Classes to the Nizam's Government of Hyderabad** to deal with the complicated issue of land reform. In the course of his work, he set up various educa-tional and other schemes for tribal peoples, all with the aim of preserving and safeguarding indigenous cultures and languages. He also accepted a teaching appointment at Osmania University, which he later relinquished, after ten years in India, to accept a lectureship at the SOAS in 1949. Within months of his initial appointment, he was made Reader and then Chair of Asian Anthropology in the School in 1951. During his 25 y ears as Professor, until

recounts an incident he was witness to while studying this small tribal community near Parantapalli in the Paloncha Samasthan of the erstwhile Hyderabad State. It seems that a *sambhar* hind wounded by pursuing hunters living on the opposite bank of the Godavari crossed over to the shallow waters on the southern bank. The tribals here, who are still considered to be among the most backward and who at best of times went mostly hungry, instead of seizing the *sambhar* drove it back to the other side as by custom the prize belonged to the first group. This quality of altruism will seldom be seen in any of our Hindu villages, where exploitation and forcible expropriation of property is a common fact of life.

The cleanliness of *Adivasi* villages and homes is a treat to ones eyes. The houses are colorfully painted and decorated, neat and clean. The surroundings are also kept clean. Even a Konda Reddi home, constructed on a raised earthen platform and made of bamboo and palm thatch is airy, neat and kept exceptionally clean. The Santhals, who make very picturesque houses, have an exceptional eye for beauty and aesthetics. They are also deeply concerned with personal hygiene and the cleanliness of their surroundings. A Santhal folk tale says "God placed rice inside a husk so it would remain clean". This is in stark contrast to homes in Hindu and Muslim dominated villages, which even in the wealthier areas of India are appallingly dirty and downright filthy. It is therefore, quite ironical, to see proposal after proposal from NGO's and other institutions seeking funding for community work in tribal areas citing the inculcation of cleanliness as among their main goals.

Tribal societies came under stress due to several other factors. Over the centuries the extension of commerce, military incursions

---

his retirement in 1976, Christoph von Fürer-Haimendorf saw the department through a period of quite exceptional growth, always encouraging his staff and students to conduct field-work as frequently and intensively as possible. He published ten ethnographic mono-graphs based on his fieldwork, including *The Chenchus* (1943), *The Reddis of the Bison Hills* (1945*)*, *The Raj Gonds of Adilabad* (1948), The *Sherpas of Nepal* (1964) and *The Konyak Nagas* (1969). He also published several other volumes of essays and theoretical works, including *Morals and merit* (1967) and *The tribes of India: struggle for survival* (1982), which drew heavily on his fieldwork.

on tribal land, and the resettling of Brahmins amidst tribal populations had an impact, as did ideological coercion or persuasion to attract key members of the tribe into "mainstream" Hindu society. This only led to many tribal communities becoming integrated into Hindu society as lower *jatis* (or castes). Quite clearly Hindu ways with their emphasis on stratification did not and still do not provide for any improvement in the status of the *Adivasis*. This and the failure of the government to provide even a modicum of development and improvement on the physical quality of life has left in its wake room for newer kinds of proselytism's. Marxism-Leninism/Maoism is one of them. The other creeping encroachment is that of the Christian missionaries who with their deep pockets and pocketbook conversions promise an exit from the material drudgery of life. Many *Adivasis* have found a good via media. Christian missionary provided education and healthcare in return for a supposed adherence to the Christian faith. Since the demand by Atal Behari Vajpayee in 1998 for a debate on conversion, the RSS and its front organizations have stepped up attacks on Christian missionaries and tried to drive them away from. The gruesome killing of the Australian missionary, the Dr. Graham Staines and his two children, which followed soon after, captured our headlines for a brief period.[60]

The failure of Government in the tribal homelands is well documented. Even the Prime Minister was forced to admit it. In the same meeting of November 27, 2009 Dr. Manmohan Singh conceded that the Indian state and establishment have abused and exploited the country's more than 80 million tribal people. "There has been a systemic failure in giving the tribal's a stake in the modern economic processes that inexorably intrude into their living spaces. The alienation built over decades is now taking a dangerous turn in some parts of our country. The systematic exploitation and social and economic abuse of our tribal communities can no longer be tolerated." The Prime Minister also said the country's authorities "must change

---

[60] **"One thousand years of Shame** " by Mohan Guruswamy in **The Indian Express,** February 3, 1999.

our ways of dealing with tribal's" and give them a "healing touch." It is "highly important," declared Singh, to integrate the tribal peoples "into the development processes… But this should not become a means of exploitation or be at the cost of their unique identity and their culture. This is the space the Naxalites are now exploiting,

A Tradition of Revolt and Resistance

The *Adivasi* revolts predate the advent of the Naxalites by more than a couple of centuries. Displaced from their homes, alienated from their lands and deprived of their resources, the tribal people have often taken to armed revolt in the past. In the Rampa region of East Godavari district more than a dozen tribal revolts occurred between 1770 and 1924. The main causes of these were the general discontent with the local administration and jagirdars, and traders and exploitation by outsiders. One revolt, between 1879 and 1916, was against the creation of forest reserves and restrictions on tribal people's access to the jungles.[61]

Alluri Sitaramaraju who became a local legend led the 1922-24 rebellion, against the restrictions on shifting cultivation, and access to forests and the tyranny of petty local officials. In Adilabad district, which has a predominant Gond population, the Bebijhari uprising in 1940 was against exploitation by non-tribal people and land alienation, and restrictions on shifting cultivation and access to forests.[62]

Elsewhere in India too the *Adivasi* ferment predates even the freedom movement. As soon as the British took over Eastern India tribal revolts broke out to challenge alien rule. In the early years of colonization, no other community in India offered such heroic resistance to British rule or faced such tragic consequences, as did the numerous *Adivasi* communities of now Jharkhand, Chhattisgarh, Orissa and Bengal. In 1772, the Paharia revolt broke out which was

---

[61] For a detailed account see "**Tribal Revolts**" by V.Raghaviah published (1971) by Andhra Rashtra Adimajati Seva Sangh, Nellore

[62] **How the tribal revolt began?** by Asha Krishnakumar in **Frontline**, Volume 21 - Issue 19, Sept. 11 - 24, 2004

followed by a five-year uprising led by Tilka Manjhi who was hanged in Bhagalpur in 1785. The Tamar and Munda revolts followed. In the next two decades, revolts took place in Singhbhum, Gumla, Birbhum, Bankura, Manbhoom and Palamau, followed by the great Kol Risings of 1832 and the Khewar and Bhumij revolts (1832-34). In 1855, the Santhals waged war against the permanent settlement of Lord Cornwallis, and a year later, numerous *Adivasi* leaders played key roles in the 1857 war of independence.

The British through massive deployment of troops quelled *Adivasi* uprisings in the Jharkhand belt across the region. The Kherwar uprising and the Birsa Munda movement were the most important of the late-18th century struggles against British rule and their local agents. The long struggle led by Birsa Munda was directed at British policies that allowed the *zamindars* and moneylenders to harshly exploit the *Adivasis*. In 1914 Jatra Oraon started what is called the Tana Movement (which drew the participation of over 25,500 Adivasis). The Tana movement joined the nation-wide Satyagraha Movement in 1920 and stopped the payment of land-taxes to the colonial Government.

During British rule, several revolts also took place in Orissa that naturally drew participation from the *Adivasis*. The significant ones included the Paik Rebellion of 1817, the Ghumsar uprisings of 1836-1856, and the Sambhalpur revolt of 1857-1864.[63]

Clearly the Government needs to think its way through this more carefully and with far greater intelligence than it has shown itself capable of so far. It must be able to distinguish *Adivasi* aspirations from Maoist intentions. The former needs to be nurtured while the later needs to be defeated. But the problem is that this is beyond the capability of the public administration apparatus we have in place now.

---

[63] Http://india_resource.tripod.com/adivasi.html

In the Heart of Darkness

If you place a map of India in front of you and put a finger on what you think is its very center then the chances are good that your finger will cover a tiny place called Multai in the Betul district of Madhya Pradesh. Over 35% of Betul district is made up of tribal's of whom the Gonds account for a quarter of the total population. The other major caste groupings are the Pawars and Kunbis, both backward castes whose economic and social condition may only be marginally better than the *Dalits* and *Adivasis.* The plight of the *Adivasis* is probably even worse in this part of the Satpura range where the deforestation is now total and what is left is a monsoon dependent arid and dusty landscape of small farms on rolling hills from which a marginal living can at best be pried out in the good years.

Multai is a small market town, about sixty kilometers south of Betul on what passes off as being a national highway that links Nagpur and Bhopal. It is also the source of the Tapti River that like the better-known Narmada flows westwards to debouch into the Arabian Sea. It's a dirty and smelly town with overflowing sewage channels and piles of cattle dung and extrusions of pig shit that make walking on the narrow lanes dicey. It's on the main north-south rail line but few trains stop here. I have driven through Multai several times over the years and had so far not even cared to stop by for a cup of tea at a roadside *dhaba.* It's that kind of place.

In the third week of November 2008 I finally stopped by at Multai and spent the good part of a week there and in the surrounding villages. What one saw was distressing and depressing. In the small village of Jhulpa (pop.495) the *sarpanch,* Radhubhai Kumre, an *adivasi* woman stated the problems with dignified brevity. There is a severe water problem and that 80% of the men had gone to Bhavnagar in Gujarat as migrant workers. Of the 550 acres owned by the villagers, only 50 acres are irrigated by wells. The rest depend on rain. Gonds comprise 60% of the population with 30% Pawars and the rest Dalits, a composition which puts them pretty low in the order of priorities of the powers that be. The village along with the neighboring village of Kondhar had received only 70 quintals of wheat under the Food for Work program. Both which together have a working population of 500 persons can thus provide work for only a hundred persons for just seven working days. She also told me that Namdev Wadbhude, the government appointed secretary of the village panchayat and a class III government employee has not showed up in the village for over two months. On the other hand whenever he determines there is work to be done, he summons the *sarpanch* to Pattan town where he lives.

The only outsiders who seem to regularly visit the village are the goons of MP's most favored excise contractor who regularly beat up the Gonds who are each allowed to distil unto 5 liters of *mahua* liquor for personal consumption. But if they distil their own booze, and maybe even sell a bit the official excise contractor, Som Distillers, loses business. The company makes significant contributions to keep the political machineries of both the major parties, the BJP and Congress, well greased and hence the police are not about to take any action on them. It was the same sorry story in village after village. Somgad, Ambori, Kondhar....

It was another story in the large village of Berul (pop.5500). The population mostly belongs to the relatively prosperous *Mali* community and the major crop of the area is cabbage. There is almost 1500 hectares under this and the farmers get a yield of about 20 tons or two truckloads per hectare. The price of Rs. 10-12000 per ha they get just about enables them to break even. This works out to 50-60 paise per kilo is nowhere near the Rs.10-12 per kilo the consumer pays, suggesting that only the middlemen prosper in the chain. The road joining Berul to Multai is in a worse state than the usual MP road, meaning there are more potholes than tarmac on it. It also means that the trucks charge more. Electricity is intermittent. The village boasts of one room government clinic and a part of the newly constructed school building recently collapsed. The villagers consider themselves fortunate that it collapsed during the night. A retired SDO who now lives here told me that he now realizes how pernicious and uncaring the system he served so long actually is. This is a prosperous village when compared to the Gond villages, but the mood of hopelessness is worse here than there.

A famous Indian (guess who?) said that the soul of India lives in its villages.[64] Some now say that Bharat lives in the villages and India in the towns. But Bharat sees India everyday for TV now reaches out almost every village where people get to see what is happening in the towns, cities and metropolises where liberalization has given the middle class a new lifestyle and where globalization is the new mantra. Will they just sit back and watch the show? Or will they be soon demanding that something comes their way also? This is the mother lode of discontent waiting to be tapped in most of India. The national political parties have other pre-occupations. It's the small regional parties and the Naxalites who are tapping this. A tourist brochure of the MP government describes the state as "the heart of India" when it would be more apt to describe it as the empty belly of India. Nevertheless if one insists that it is the heart of India, it must be its heart of darkness.

What is to be done?[65]

There is no need to seek solutions in VI Lenin's prescriptions. And for that matter in Mao Zedong's. Solutions lie within the Indian Constitution and in the universal principles of justice and equality. In

---

[64] **"The soul of India lives in its villages",** declared M. K. Gandhi at the beginning of 20th century. According to the 2001 Indian census, 74% of Indians live in 638,365 different villages. The size of these villages varies considerably. 236,004 Indian villages have a population less than 500, while 3,976 villages have a population of 10,000+.

[65] **"What Is to Be Done**?" was a political pamphlet, written by VI Lenin at the end of 1901 and early 1902. A novel by Nikolai Chernyshevsky with the same name inspired the title. The piece called for the formation of a revolutionary vanguardist party that would direct the efforts of the working class. Lenin thought that left to their own devices, workers would be merely satisfied with "trade unionism and that only a revolutionary party could direct a "scientific" socialist revolution."The history of all countries shows," he wrote, "that the working class, exclusively by its own efforts, is able to develop only trade-union consciousness," that is, combining into unions, etc. Social ism, however, is the product of the intellectuals. The piece partly precipitated the split of the Russian Social Democratic Party (RSDLP) between the Bolsheviks and Mensheviks. The former became Lenin's revolutionary party, while the latter preferred to take a more moderate path to liberal government that they hoped might eventually lead to socialist revolution.

the early days of our Republic, Jawaharlal Nehru on the advice of people like Verrier Elwin sought to insulate the tribal areas from the predations of the new order that was emerging in India. The migration of outsiders into the traditional *adivasi* homelands continues unabated. This need to be reversed and the census data that will be available after the currently underway Census of India will provide enough information about who is a local person and who is an outsider. There are 332 tribal majority *tehsils*[66] in India, of which 110 are in the Northeast. Thus we see that in as many as 222 *tehsils* spanning a population of over 20 million.[67] This is just a quarter of the total number of tribal people in India.

The Fifth and Sixth Schedules under Article 244 of the Indian Constitution in 1950 provided for self-governance in specified tribal majority areas.[68] In 1999 the Government of India even issued a draft National Policy on Tribals[69] to address the developmental needs of tribal people. Special emphasis was laid on education, forestry,

---

[66] A **tehsil** also known as **tahsil, tahasil, taluka, taluk, taluq,** and **mandal)** is an administrative division, also known as a sub-division in some states. Generally, a tehsil consists of a city or <u>town</u> that serves as its *headquarters*, possibly additional towns, and a number of villages. As an entity of local government, it exercises certain fiscal and administrative powers over the village panchayat's and municipalcouncils within its jurisdiction. It is the ultimate executive agency for land records and related administrative matters. Its chief official is usual ly called the tehsildar.

[67] **An Atlas of Tribal India** : With Computed T ables of District-Lev el Data and Its Geographical Interpretation (Hardcover) by~ Moonis Raza and Aijazuddin Ahmed. New Delhi: Concept Pub. Co. , 1990.

[68] The Fifth Schedule of the Indian Constitution ('the Fifth Schedule') provides for the administration and control of tribal lands (termed 'scheduled areas') within nine states of India. The Fifth Schedule provides protection to the Adivasi (tribal) people living in scheduled areas from alienation of their lands and natural resources to non-tribals. This constitutional safeguard is now under imminent threat of being amended to effect transfer of tribal lands to non-tribals and corporate bodies. This move has serious implications for the very survival and culture of the millions of tribal people in India. The Fifth Schedule covers Tribal ar eas in 9 states of I ndia namely Andhr a Pradesh, Jharkhand, Gujarat, Himachal Pradesh, Maharashtra, Madhya Pradesh, Chhattisgarh, Orissa and Rajasthan.

[69] The Indian government has released a **draft national policy on tribals** to address the issue of developing this section of the population in "an integr ated and holistic manner ". For the first time since the formation of the Indian republic, 60 years ago, the**Ministry of Tribal Affairs** released the draft document whose aim is to "uplift the tribals who have been facing acute pov erty, alienation from land and lack of l ivelihood opportunities," in many parts of India. The document was released in New Delhi on July 21, 2006.

healthcare, languages, resettlement and land rights. The NDA government even established a Ministry of Tribal Affairs. The draft was meant to be circulated between MP's, MLA's and Civil Society groups. A Cabinet Committee on Tribal Affairs was meant to constantly review the policy. Little has happened since. The draft policy is still a draft, which means there is no policy. But it must also be stated that this sudden concern for tribals was mostly motivated by the fears of conversion to Christianity that would have precluded their assimilation into the Hindu samaj. Thus, even though the states of Chattisgarh and Jharkhand were carved out of Bihar and Madhya Pradesh, real tribal issues relating to their culture, way of life and aspirations were not addressed. Not to be left behind the UPA government drafted the Scheduled Tribes (Recognition of Forest Rights) Bill in 2005 but did not act upon it due to pressure mounted by wildlife activists and the wildlife tourism lobby.

But there are several paradoxes that must also be dealt with first.[70] The most important of these is that to provide good government in the worst of law and order environments. A better civil administration structure must come up in place of the one present. This means the best officers drawn from across the country. Perhaps it is time to constitute a new All India Service, similar to the former Indian Frontier Administrative Service. The IFAS was an eclectic group of officers drawn from various arms of the government. Unfortunately it was merged into the IAS.[71] All tribal majority areas

---

[70] Chandigarh, April 9 (IANS) **Vice President M. Hamid Ansari** said "The public domain is witnessing a debate on the crisis of governance in the country in recent years and the focus of this debate is on the ethical dimension of it. The palpable public disenchantment with it (governance) has directed the focus of the debate on the ethical dimension of the framework of governance. This too is reflected in the report of the second Administrative Reforms Commission, which begins with a candid acknowledgement that governance is the weak link in our quest for prosperit y and equity,"

[71] A special service known as the **Indian Frontier Administrative Service** was established in 1957, to administer the Northeastern states. This service was doing a commendable job of adequately administering the Northeastern states with due regard to cultural and tribal sensitivities of the people. For reasons best known to the government, the Indian Frontier Administrative Service was abolished in the later half of the sixties and merged into the IAS.

must be consolidated into administrative divisions whose authority must be vested with democratically chosen leadership. This body could be called the Adivasi Maha-panchayat and must function as a largely autonomous institution. All laws passed by the state legislatures must be ratified to the satisfaction of the Maha-panchayat. Instead of the state capital controlled government, the instruments of public administration dealing with education, health, irrigation, roads and land records must be handed over to local government structures. The police must also be made answerable to local elected officials and not be a law unto themselves. The lament of the *Adivasi* about their role in their government is well known. It is the subject of many a folk song.[72]

The local community must get all the royalties for the minerals extracted from their areas. Till recently the royalty paid by the extractors was a meager Rs.27 per metric ton. It has now been raised to 10% of the market price.[73] The cost of extraction is estimated to be not more than Rs.250 per ton. The export price has never fallen below Rs. 1500 per ton In February 2010 the landed price per ton of Indian iron ore in China was $128, which is over Rs.6000 per ton.[74] So one can imagine the margins the private and state owned exporters are raking in. Similar advantages are also accruing the Indian producers of steel, like Tata Steel and the state owned SAIL.

---

[72] "And the Gods were greatly troubled/ in their heavenly courts and councils/ Sat no Gods of Gonds among them. / Gods of other nations sat there/ Eighteen threshing-floors of Brahmins/ Sixteen scores of Telinganas/ But no Gods of Gonds appeared there/ From the Glens of Seven Mountains/ From the twelve hills of the valleys." Page 151, from a song of the Pardhans or bards of the Gonds. Translated by Captain J. Forsyth in" **The Highlands of Central India**" reprint published in 1996 by Asian Educational Services. Original published by Chapman and Hall, Ltd., London 1919. ISBN 81-206-1159-4

[73] The **CCEA** has approved 10 per cent royalty on iron ore. Royalty rates on many other minerals have also been revised. A formal notification for the same is likely to be issued in a day on two," a top mines ministry official told PTI. "The government is likely to earn Rs 4,629 crore from the changes in the royalty structure based on the production levels of 2007-08," he said. In 2007-08, the government had earned an estimated Rs 2,280 crore . Last fiscal's details could not be ascertained. Press Trust of India / New Delhi August 12, 2009.

[74] **"Iron'ic? Story of the Great Indian Loot."** By Shankar Raghuraman in **The Times of India**, Hyderabad, June 5, 2010

But the real problem is that this relatively small amount of over Rs.4600 crores because of the enhanced royalty will accrue to the state government's coffers and like before little will filter down. It now needs to be mandated by law that for minerals extracted in tribal areas the royalty received should be entirely earmarked to the local administration. Only the *Adivasi* Maha-panchayat should be vested with the power to give mineral exploitation licenses to corporations.

If land is required for industrialization, the prices must be fixed to the satisfaction of local government authorities and not arbitrarily set by distant bureaucrats to suit the convenience of the investing corporation. We cannot have any more episodes like that in Kalinga Nagar[75] where the Tata's got *Adivasi* lands at a fraction of their market value. Tata's and others now want to exploit Bastar's iron ore. We have before us the experience of the National Mineral Development Corporation's giant iron ore extraction project at Bailladilla in Bastar's Dantewara district. The locals get nothing but the most menial jobs and in return their hitherto pristine environment is ravaged beyond recognition with the streams choked with the debris of excavation. In 2007 the Andhra Pradesh government, in complete contravention of the laws governing the conversion of notified forests and tribal homelands and in a total reversal of the pre-election commitments of the Congress party, has signed agreements with Jindal South West (JSW) of the Jindal group and the Anrak company of Ras-al-Khaimah to mine bauxite in the picturesque Araku Valley in the eastern district of Vizagapatam. This is estimated to displace over

---

[75] **Tata Steel** signed a memorandum of understanding with the Orissa government for the Kalingnagar project in November 2004. More than five years on, 300 families are yet to be moved from the site.

The project saw violent agitation against land acquisition in 2006, when police firing killed 14 tribals. Human rights activists have blamed industrial projects for displacing tribal's, a cause taken up by Naxali tes on a war f ooting, literally. According to a recent Ci tigroup report, tribals are among the biggest victims of displacement. Although they comprise nine per cent of the population, their land is 40 per cent of the land acquired till date.

Nerurkar admitted the Naxalite movements had local support. "There is a dissatisfied lot," he said. "Tata Steel w ants to adjust to this issue b y working wi th the communities. W e have been doing this for 100 years and wil l continue to do i t."

100,000 tribals while creating jobs for a mere four hundred. The state government expects to receive a royalty of Rs. 64.5 crores while the two companies are slated to rake in Rs. 1260 crores and Rs. 2350 crores respectively.[76] Clearly this kind of exploitation of tribal homelands and loot of the state has got to stop. And above all if natural resources must be exploited, then the local communities which bear the brunt of the suffering and burden due to displacement and pollution must benefit the most. This is possible only when the public administration system is decentralized to ensure that local governments feel responsible for their people. That is why the Fifth and Sixth schedules under Article 244 of the Indian Constitution were enshrined in it in 1950. Clearly sixty years is long enough to give the provisions of the Constitution life?

Another manifestation of civilization here has been the incidence of venereal diseases and the numbers of children fathered by NMDC employees who exploit liberal adivasi values. Clearly we need a new paradigm of development to work here. Merely establishing a "plantation" does not develop an area. In return for their land, heritage and sheer cultural assault on their mores and values, the poor Maria Gonds of the region have got nothing. Sure India needs more iron ore, but people like the Tata's must be made to pay a price commensurate with the costs they will impose. If hydrocarbon reserves are opened to exploitation to the highest bidder, surely a similar and possible more equitable way can be found for the extraction of other mineral wealth? Just like Mr. Ratan Tata pays full value for acquiring Corus or Jaguar, he must now learn to pay full value to the people of the region who own the land. Mr. Tata will do well to visit an Indian reservation in the USA, where the community now gets top dollar prices for their resources.

When Dr. Manmohan Singh first became Prime Minister, he promised that the reform of government was his number one priority.

---

[76] **"Development? 1 L to lose land, jobs for 400."** By G.Arun Kumar in **The Times of India**, Hyderabad on June 5, 2010.

He promised us a government by the people and for the people. Instead of devoting himself to this he seems to have frittered his time schmoozing with the fat cats of the CII and World Economic Forum and running a government for them alone.

In the life of a nation, things are never too late. Changes in course can always be charted. All that is needed is to realize that State is floundering and that it has made huge mistakes perpetrated huge injustices and has inflicted huge sufferings on tens of millions. The people who are vested with the control of the State must have the humility to realize this. It's never too late for a new beginning. But first the Prime Minister of India must have the bigness of heart to beg the forgiveness of India's *Adivasi* people and seek a new beginning.

Non-State Actors Operating in Indian Hinterland

Vinita Priyedarshi

With insurgency growing in importance as a national security problem[1], it has led to new interest in analysing this concept and coming to suggestions as to how best this threat could be met by the affected states. The issue has assumed significance considering that 33 districts of various states of India have been declared as severely affected by left-wing extremism with Naxalites having spread their tentacles to 22 states in varying degrees.

This paper makes an attempt to analyse the growth of the movement in the rural hinterland for an in-depth analysis of the phenomenon of Left-Wing-Extremism (LWE) in India. The paper's focus would be on the analysis of the ideology of LWE in India and the strategy and tactics adopted by them. Further the paper would discuss the organizational set up followed by Maoists in India. Last but not the least; the paper would discuss the strategy pursued by the Government in dealing with left-wing extremism while suggesting ways and means of improving them.

---

[1] During 2006, f rom the peripheries of Andhr a Pr adesh, Bihar, Chat tisgarh, Jharkhand, Orissa, Maharashtra, West Bengal etc, the Naxalite conflict came to be recognized as the 'single biggest internal security challenge ever faced' by India (Asian Centre for Human Rights: 2007:2)

Ideology, Strategy and Tactics of Left-Wing Extremism (LWE)

Left wing extremism (LWE), based on the belief that terrorism is the only strategy of revolutionary movement for the weak in the Third World emerged in Europe and elsewhere especially since the late 1950s. LWE or Naxalism as it is called in India traces its roots to a village called Naxalbari in West Bengal. The movement was started in 1967 by an extremists' break-away faction of the CPM under the charismatic leadership of Charu Mazumdar.

Charu Mazumdar was greatly influenced by the Maoist ideology and wanted to bring about an armed revolution based on Chinese Communists' ideology and methods which led them to victory in China (In fact, during the height of Cultural Revolution in China, People's Daily described the uprising of May 1967 in India as "a pearl of spring thunder"). However the death of Mazumdar in a police station in July 1972 led to a temporary collapse of the movement leading to the many splits and mergers in the Naxalite groupings and left wing parties.

However, the merger of the two major Maoists parties i.e. People's War Group (PWG) and Maoist Communist Centre (MCC) into CPI (Maoist) in 2004 marked the beginning of a new era in the Naxalite phenomenon with the new found CPI (M) representing the New Democratic Revolution. The merger has in no way changed the original goals of the organization which is to establish a 'compact liberated zone', an area of control that would extend from the Nepalese border to Andhra Pradesh in the south.[2]

Soon after its formation the CPI (M) issued a document titled 'Party Programme' laying down the ideological basis of the merged entity. The document holds that there are four major contradictions in our country, namely Contradiction between imperialism and Indian

---

[2] The compact revolutionary zone by Sanjay K Jha, source: http://www.outlookindia.com/article.aspx?219318

people; Contradiction between feudalism and the broad masses of the people; Contradiction between capital and labour; and Contradiction among the ruling classes out of which the first two contradictions are basic contradictions. These two contradictions have to be resolved during the present stage of the New Democratic Revolution. Maoists envision that the New Democratic Revolution will smash the imperialist and feudal ideology and culture of the present society and will establish the new democratic culture and a socialist ideology in its place. During the last phase of the so called New Democratic Revolution Maoists aim to build a united front comprising the four-class- the working class, peasantry, petty bourgeoisie and national bourgeoisie-under the leadership of working class based upon worker-peasant alliance.

The Party manifesto of the CPI (M) lays down a three pronged strategy (termed as the three 'magic weapons') for the achievement of their stated ideology which includes a strong revolutionary party based on Marxism-Leninism-Maoism as its guiding ideological basis in all matters, a strong and well-disciplined people's army under the leadership of such a party; and a united front of all revolutionary classes under the leadership of the proletariat based on worker-peasant alliance and on the general programme of people's democratic revolution.

Naxalites, to give practical shape to their stated ideology and strategy have been following the basic tenet of Mao that 'power grows out of barrel of the gun' which was clearly reiterated in their Congress held in 2007 where they resolved   to intensify the people's war and to take the war to all fronts. To attain their stated ideology the Maoists have followed a well laid out strategy and one of the important elements of this strategy has been to oppose through calculated violence the establishment of Special Economic Zones (SEZs) which they consider as   neo-colonial enclaves on Indian Territory.

Another element of Naxalite strategy has been to disrupt the elections to stall the democratic exercise (especially in Chhatisgarh,

Jharkhand, Orissa and Bihar).

As a part of the larger strategy, Maoists also enforce economic blockades some of them inspired by several strikes organized by the Maoist party in Nepal. Naxals have carried out blockades on several occasions. On such occasions train services across the states have been adversely affected.

For giving practical shape to their strategy, the Naxalites have continuously been engaged in innovation of the tactics adopted by them. They have even resorted to repeating some of their tactics of the 1969- 72 periods of attacking their political opponents in addition to the police. Meanwhile the Maoists have developed some expertise in the use of landmines and Improvised Explosive Devices (IEDs) which has been responsible for significant casualties among police and other security personnel. Quite recently the Naxalites trapped and gunned down 75 Central Reserve Police Force (CRPF) and State Police personnel in the thick forests of Mukrana in Dantewada district of Chhattisgarh on 6th April 2010 followed by the killing of 35 people, (24 civilians and 11 SPOs) when the Naxalites blew up a bus in Dantewada on 17th of April 2010. The incident was quickly followed by the killing of four CRPF personnel in a landmine attack in West Bengal's West Midnapore District on 19th of April.

There has been an increasing militarisation and simultaneous acquisition of sophisticated firearms and ammunitions by the Naxlites. Their arsenal now boasts of self-loading rifles (SLRs), AK series of rifles and INSAS rifles. It is believed that currently the Maoists have also gained access to the technology of fabricating rockets and rocket launchers.

Organizational Structure of PWG

As far as the organizational structure of the PWG (which is the main representative of CPI-M in the current era) is concerned it consists of six military platoons, 28 area committees, 66 local guerrilla squads, and 16 action teams. Apart from the CPI (M) State Committees, there are three Special Zonal Committees covering the strategic areas around the Godavari River, north Telangana, Dandakaranya and Andhra- Orrissa Border.

The PWG lays down that the People's Guerrilla Army (PLA) would consist of a main force, a secondary force, and a people's militia. The PLA is organised into platoons who are divided into two: the military platoon and the protection platoon. The main fighting platoon comprises of trained guerrillas who are further divided into sections and sub-sections. The *dalam* or armed squad is the secondary fighting unit whose strength varies from time to time. The squad mostly functions as Local Guerrilla Squad (LGS), however in some areas it is organised as Central Guerrilla Squad (CGS). The fighting force of the PWG is known as People's Guerrilla Army which was formed in the year 2000.

Government Counter-Strategy

Approach of the governments at both centre and state level has been based on three pillars of strengthening the police forces, promoting development and improving the socio-economic conditions of the affected areas through a number of schemes.

In March 2006, the then Union Home Minister announced a 14-point strategy to deal with the Naxal problem in which the Government accepted that Naxalism is not merely law and order problem and therefore needs to be addressed comprehensively through political, security, development and public perception management in a holistic manner. Collective and coordinated approach, improved police response and no dialogue with the Naxalites unless they agree to give up violence and arms were some of the points stressed in the strategy document which till date remains the corner-stone of Government's Counter-Naxalite strategy. As the current counter-Naxal strategy announced by Mr Chidambaram, Central para-military forces have been provided to the affected States, including Chhattisgarh, to help the State Governments carry out counter-insurgency operations, regain control of areas dominated by the Naxalites, restore the civil administration, and re-start development work[3]. Virtually ruling out any role for the Army for now, Chidambaram made it clear that the CRPF will lead the charge. Even the security forces charged with the responsibility of guarding the borders will not have any role in the anti-Naxal offensive[4].

An 'Empowered Group' of Ministers headed by the Home Minister has been constituted to overcome the difficulties of coordination between the state governments and the centre. The Group has been assigned the task of closely monitoring the spread of Naxal movement, reviewing special measures to be taken in improving inter-state coordination and exchange of intelligence, personnel and any other kind of assistance.

An inter-ministerial group has also been formed to review and coordinate work being done for providing livelihood and amenities to the deprived population. Ministries of rural development, environment and forests, Panchayati Raj and Planning Commission have their representatives on the committee with the main objective of bringing the alienated people into the mainstream.

Development and security have been merged under the aegis of Naxal Management Division in the Union Home Ministry. It monitors the naxal situation and counter-measures being taken by the affected States with the objective of improving ground-level policing and development response as per the location specific action plans formulated/to be formulated by the affected States. It also reviews proper implementation of various developmental schemes of Ministries/Departments concerned in the Naxal affected areas as also optimum utilisation of funds released under such schemes.

---

[3] Chidamabaram vows to lead anti-Naxal fight, source: http://arabnews.com/world/article43963.ece

[4] Ibid.

Further, since Naxal problem has a deep connection with the tribal and forested areas, the government has been making efforts on the legislation front also in the direction of recognizing the right of forest dwellers on the forest produce. Other important area on which Central government has been pushing the states is in introducing land reforms which remains a political issue and various states have implemented the land reforms with mixed success.

The Governemnt has also proposed to form a National Counter Terrorism Centre to coordinate operations,   intelligence and anti-terror steps at the national level. The aim of the Centre would be to ensure organise a centralized agency for collection and collation of intelligence and enhanced information sharing and intelligence on real-time basis with   improved net-centric information command structure[5].

A special counter-insurgency force of central para-military forces designated COBRA is also being raised to counter Naxal force. Naxal affected states have even been sanctioned India Reserve battalions not only to strengthen security apparatus but also to wean away the youth from rebel activity by providing them with gainful employment.

Training of police force is another facet which has been receiving greater attention in states like AP and Chattisgarh which are imparting special training to counter the well trained and motivated Naxal guerrillas and fighters. In the backdrop of major attacks by Maoists against paramilitary and central police personnel, the Army has proposed to set up a dedicated centre to ready the security men for the battle against the Naxals[6].

In the light of the renewed attack by the CPI-M the security forces and Chief Ministers of Bengal, Andhra Pradesh, Maharashtra,

---

[5] A super ministry of securi   ty, sour ce: ht tp://indiatoday.intoday.in/site/Story/78193/Na-tion/A+super+ministry+of+security.html

[6] Army proposes new anti-Naxal training centre, source: http://www.zeenews.com/news627622.html

Chhattisgarh and Orissa have all asked for air-support in the words of Home Minister P Chidambaram which the Minister has shown reluctance in accepting, owing to the limited mandate received by him[7].

Recommendations

Despite all good efforts put by the central and the state Government the Naxalite movement has refused to subside. In fact there has been sudden upsurge in the Naxalite violence in the wake of Home Minster P Chidamabaram's new policy of coordinated offensive against the Naxalites under 'Operation Green Hunt'. The effort here is to evaluate the gaps visible in the Government's strategy in dealing with the Naxalites and suggest changes which need to be incorporated in it.

So far the counter-insurgency strategy has focussed on the use of paramilitary forces or the raising of Special Task Forces like the Greyhounds or the Cobras. Time and again by the security analysts and experts have said that in any counter-insurgency it should be the state police forces which should be in the forefront of fighting. They know the culture, the ethos, the language of the people and thus have a bond with the people. Since they know their past and are in their present, they are better equipped to handle them. The defeat of Naxalism in Andhra Pradesh and terrorism in Punjab reveals that leadership of the local state police forces have paid positive dividends. Even in Gadchiroli (which has suffered least casualty ever since Operation Green Hunt began) reports suggest that CRPF troops always moved in tandem with the Maharashtra police; all operations had at least 30 per cent from the state police and there was increased intelligence-sharing and verification between the CRPF and the local police[8].

---

[7] Need to revisit anti-Naxal strategy: Chidambaram, source: http://news.outlookindia.com/item.aspx?682391

[8] As reported in the Indian Express, **April 20, 2010.**

While the counter-insurgency forces are restricted by the jurisdictions of the state no such restrictions apply to the Naxalites. Any advance on part of the central government to enter into the jurisdiction of the state is viewed with suspicion. Besides each state is governed by its own dynamics of internal politics which might be at variance with the rules governing the politics at the national level. Under the scenario it seems more viable to educate the state governments of the benefits of raising Special anti-Naxalite forces and providing assistance to them in doing so. Such a strategy is more likely to get approval by the states since such forces would be under the jurisdiction of the state and it also bears additional advantage of creation of a permanent pool of trained police forces which could be used in counter-terrorism and other internal security matters as well.

Intelligence which forms the back-bone of any counter-insurgency becomes a herculean task for forces like army or CRPF which are not well versed with the language and people of the region and who are seen as alien forces by the local masses. Further deployment of CRPF or Army carries with it the problem of coordination between the centre and the state considering the fact the internal security fall within the jurisdiction of the states. Their role, as the CRPF's commander of anti-Naxal operations, Vijay Raman, says, is of "a force multiplier, not contractors to have been given the job of exclusively rooting out Naxals[9]." It is interesting to note that in Andhra Pradesh, which is being projected as a success model, even at the peak of counter-insurgency phase in 2005-2009, merely six battalions of paramilitary forces were ever deployed for anti-Naxalite operations[10].

Proper leadership at the higher level of police apparatus is vital in any counter-insurgency. Yet going by the analysis of Ajai Sahni

---

[9] Ibid.

[10] The data has been taken from an article by Ajai Sahni in 'Seminar' on "Dreamscape of 'solutions'".

(counter-terrorist and counter-insurgency expert) there is huge deficit in the ratio of DSP to SSP (deficits in Andhra Pradesh stands at 19 %, Bihar 35 %, Chattisgarh 28 %, Jharkhand 51 %, Orissa 34 % and West Bengal 25 %) as also in the ratio of Assistant Sub-Inspector to Inspector (Andhra Pradesh 15 %, Bihar 39 %, Chattisgarh 41 %, Jharkhand 18 %, Orissa 34 % and West Bengal 30 %). The 13th Finance commission has allotted adequate funds for modernisation of police forces and yet it would take time before a pool of trained police forces having professional leadership could become operational.

The type of training and amount of forces which should be deployed in counter-insurgency operations also needs to be given proper thought. The training of state police forces should include the basics of fighting jungle warfare. However, there are other factors like the strategy of the adversary, the preparedness of the adversary, the resources available to the security forces, the intelligence which is available to the forces and the terrain in which the operations has to be conducted which together will determine the strategy as well operational tactic of the counter-insurgency forces.

Although the government counter-insurgency policy does talk about the creation of a perception management cell which would frame the overall policy of articulation of its views and policies to the masses, it has not yet been implemented. Offer of dialogue has been made without chalking out a strategy as to how it should react to the Naxalites rejection of dialogue or how it should utilise the ceasefire period once the negotiations commences. It is recommended therefore that the following strategic imperatives should be given adequate considerations in any dialogue with the insurgents.

There is no denying the fact that Naxalism owes its origin to lack of governmental authority in tribal hinterland and its failure in looking after the basic needs of the tribals. There is an urgent need of connecting the interiors with the mainland through proper roads. Construction of roads needs to be supplemented by the building of public utilities like hospitals and schools. Protection of these public places shouldn't be left to security forces alone but it would be wiser to involve group of villagers who could take turn in guarding them. Involvement of villagers might dissuade the Naxalites from attacking these places.

Corruption in all ranks and file has led to siphoning of the money meant for the development of the tribals as well as denial of their basic rights. The government needs to overhaul the administration particularly those involved in the implementation of the policies related to the tribals. Proper implementation of land tenancy rights as well as memorandum of understating with the mining corporate is long overdue. The laws are there, the need is the political will to implement it keeping aside the compulsions of power politics.

Session III

Suggested Strategies

Chairman   -   Lt Gen P K Singh,
                 PVSM, AVSM (Retd)
                 Director USI

Speakers   -   Lt Gen V G Patankar,
                 PVSM, UYSM, VSM (Retd)

            -    Ajit Doval, IPS (Retd)

A MILITARY STRATEGY TO COUNTER TERRORISM

Lt Gen VG Patankar (Retd)

Introduction

History is replete with examples of use of terror, violence and intimidation, usually by underground or revolutionary groups against the state, to achieve a political end. For such groups, it was a tactical necessity because of the asymmetry that existed between their capabilities and those of the state. However, with some states choosing to employ terror as a weapon against another state, the concept has transcended into the realm of strategy and a new form of warfare; it is sometimes referred to as 'state sponsored terrorism'.

It is not difficult to see why terrorism is increasingly becoming the preferred form of warfare. While ownership of terrorist outfits can remain with individuals or organisations, states (i.e., governments) have the ability to manipulate them to their geo-political advantage both in strategic and tactical terms. It is a low cost option; expenditure on providing logistics support to even a large terrorist organisation is much lower than that incurred in maintaining large combat forces on active duty. Some funding could even be received from other states that support a common cause. It has low political costs because governments can easily disown terrorists as 'non-state actors' (NSA) acting on their own.

Terrorism is, therefore, firmly established as a potent threat to the security of a nation. For us in India it has been, and is likely to continue to be, a major threat to our national security. Furthermore, we face different types of threats of terrorism. They could be classified into two main types; one that is indigenous and the other is one which is induced, aided and abetted externally. We are up against both; 'Jihadi' terrorism that comes mainly from Pakistani terrorist groups that have government patronage and the other from Naxals/ Left wing extremists (also called Maoist).

Analysis of the Threat

Before formulating a military strategy against terrorism, it is important to understand the precise nature of the threat with a view to first creating a doctrine to deal with it. It involves defining the problem and analysing the threat in detail.

Terrorism is sponsored by states like Pakistan, who make no secret of its animosity towards India, as well as the non-state actors whose actions are inimical to our security interests. For our enemies terrorism is the clever, low cost strategy that has high potential for haemorrhaging our peace and progress. It is a type of warfare that may appear to be in the realm of low intensity operations but it cannot be treated as such because it has the potential to escalate rapidly. If nipped in the bud, a counter-terrorist operation could be just a police mission (as in the case of the recent Times Square episode in New York). Once launched in full scale (eg attack on Lok Sabha on 13 December 2001 or the infamous '26/11' at Mumbai in November 2008), it could precipitate into war or near war-like situation. With the increasing possibilities of terrorists gaining, or being given access to weapons of mass destruction (even a dirty bomb), it could reach the maximum intensity operations known to mankind.

Left wing extremists or Naxalist have taken to terrorism for tactical reasons. Their aim is to inflict maximum damage on governmental institutions including the administration and security forces so as to demonstrate their capabilities and resolve. As in most insurgencies, their activities are driven by ideological orientation and are aimed at replacing existing system of governance through revolution. The success achieved by the Maoists in Nepal is perhaps the most recent example in our neighbourhood of what could be accomplished using terrorist methods. It would have, without doubt, encouraged indigenous left wing extremists in various parts of India.

Targets of terrorist attacks are usually physical; like important persons, sensitive installations, vital systems that run large scale operations like the railways, air services, ports and so on. The greater objectives, on the other hand, are to cause immeasurable impact on economy, military capabilities and national morale. Domino effect of such impact could easily result in collapse of governments, dislocation of public life, destruction of virtual infrastructure like e-banking and various cyber networks; causing colossal economic losses and immense hardships to the nation as a whole. This is no different from the likely after effects of a full scale war.

FORMULATING A STRATEGY

A National Doctrine

Fundamentally terrorists plan their activities to instil fear in the minds of their targets. Shock action and ruthlessness of attacks are essential ingredients of their strikes. By choosing the time, place and intention of their attacks carefully and preparing themselves well, they aim to achieve high degree of success. Unless the plot is unearthed and suppressed before it is unleashed, it is very seldom that any terrorist attack is a complete failure. Repeated successes for the terrorists and comparative ineffectiveness of government machinery could lead to a sense of despondency and uncertainty among the target population. Such a state of mind enhances the fear-factor; I choose to call it the 'Gabbar Singh[1]' syndrome!

---

[1] After the infamous villain, in the hugely popular film 'Sholay', who had terrorised the local area.

The leadership of terrorist organisations (whether internally or externally driven, abetted or sponsored) may well be highly motivated and may be expected to make even the ultimate sacrifice in the pursuit of its goals, or perceived cause. The core of the organisation may also constitute individuals whose dedication could be fanatical. However, there are two areas of weakness in every terrorist organisation; firstly, the majority of its rank and file are not as motivated or so highly charged with the mission as the leadership and secondly, terrorist organisations can be self-sustaining only for financial support at best; that too depending upon the level of donor support. For the rest, including launching strikes, it has to depend on external support. External links could be the 'Achilles Heel'.

Among those terrorists that are not highly motivated, there are those who may have enlisted after being carried away by emotional exhortations and effective propaganda. Over period of time, particularly as the full implications of continued commitment to terrorist ideology become clear, the motivation tends to wane. There are yet others whose participation is purely mercenary in character; they are simply in it for the money or personal gains (such as settling personal scores or for vendetta). They too are not the do-or-die type and hence a weak link.

External support required is of various types. To begin with, terrorist organisations need a steady inflow of new recruits. Funding and logistic support is also vital. For all this willing and enthusiastic collaboration of the people is essential. Some tend to do so out because of conviction, some out of misplaced sense of loyalty but many opportunists do so out of greed – for money or power or both. The latter could be compromised to make inroads into terrorist organisation.

For support, terrorist groups, including Naxal groups, also need to establish temporary or long term links for training, equipment or logistic support. Such links are established less on ideological grounds but more for expediency and in the majority of cases have nexus with small and large criminal elements (mafia outfits operating international rackets involving smuggling of drugs, arms, human trafficking and so on). Such outfits also have their weak spots that could be exploited.

Any doctrine to defeat terrorism should be able to deal with the various manifestations of the threats. It should aim to exploit the two areas of weakness mentioned above. Two major principles emerge:-

(a) Security forces can defeat terrorists; however, terrorism can be defeated only by the people.

(b) External support of every kind is like oxygen to any terrorist organisation; any disruption in its flow would choke it fatally. In other words, it is the jugular that needs to be severed.

It is axiomatic that a doctrine to fight terrorism should be based on defeating everything that the terrorists aim to achieve. It cannot simply be an anti-thesis of all known terrorist ideologies in general. It should be aimed at defeating all perceived objectives of specific terrorist organisations. Thus there should be a doctrine to deal with all Naxal/ left wing terrorist outfits operating in various states of our country and another to deal with all Pakistan-based terror groups like LeT, JeM and their counterparts or partners in India such as SIMI, Indian Mujahideen and so on. Both doctrines should have the following common elements: -

(a) People (or the target population) should be the centre of gravity.

(b) The Government should never appear to be the weaker protagonist or deal with the terrorist from a position of weakness, no matter how grave the threat. (This includes cases of hostage taking, hijacking of aeroplanes etc).

(c) The government should not compromise on the fundamental premise of the constitution, which should be inviolable. It could, however, show willingness to consider genuine grievances strictly within the constitutional framework.

(d) Just as the State deals with a military aggression through its own military means, so it should deal with intimidation. It should adopt every means to show its capability to counter intimidation. This can be done very effectively by instituting strong credible deterrence. Swift retribution, punitive strikes, effecting sanctions are various ways of making deterrence credible. In so doing, a bit of over-reaction is better than a weak-kneed, confused whimper or no reaction at all.

(e) If terrorists choose to adopt unconventional methods to strike, it is naïve and outright irrational to counter them through conventional means. We should 'Fight a terrorist like a terrorist' and a terrorist state in equal terms (different from state-sponsored terrorism).Policy of turning the other cheek will not work with those who do not honour law of the land and accepted norms of social behaviour; rogues are best subdued by rogue methods.

(f) All components and instruments of government must act in unison. All ministries and departments of both at the central as well as state governments should follow similar norms and policies and each must be supportive of the other. This can be best achieved by common resolve and unity of command.

(g) Command must travel vertically up or down. In an escalating situation it should seamlessly pass to the next higher echelon of command. Similarly as it gradually begins to return to normal, it must be passed down till status quo ante resumes. Resources and elements of higher echelon must commensurately disengage and withdraw.

A Few Axioms:-

(a) Better to be guilty of commission (action) than omission (inaction).

(b) Not only should one "speak softly but carry a big stick"; once a while use the big stick to show the adversary you know how to use it and HAVE THE WILL TO DO SO.

A MILITARY STRATEGY

Although it is important to have specific military strategies to deal with Naxals and for terrorist groups sponsored by countries inimical to India's interests, there are many aspects in the two that are common. They are listed below.

(a) Overt strategy parts of which could be in the public domain (unclassified) and rest would be classified.

(b) Covert strategy which would be highly classified.

(c) Counter-terrorist operations should be essentially based on the principle of 'a velvet fist in an iron glove'. The strategy must distinguish between the people and the terrorists.

(d) A military strategy should be but a part of overall national strategy. It should not only complement it but should in fact run concurrent with it.

(e) This is essentially a battle for the hearts and minds and NOT for elimination of all terrorists because as with Naxals many other terrorists would be Indian citizens who deserve to be given an opportunity to abjure violence and return to the society. Military operations should, therefore, be 'people-friendly'. It does not detract from the basic principle that terrorists should be dealt with for their acts of commission or infringement of human rights as proscribed by law.

(f) Assuming that the military would get involved in counter terrorist operations only after all other means have failed, it should be done according to a well thought out 'entry' and exit' policy (not 'strategy') which should be clearly articulated. Manifestation of the policy should be visible to not only the people but also the Naxals. This is best done by clearly achievable and identified bench-marks.

(g) The first task should be to bring situation to status quo ante[2] at the earliest. The military should be engaged for the shortest possible duration after which the central police organizations (CPO) and state administration should quickly take over. Finally, as normalcy is restored, CPO too should leave handing over the task of re-establishing law and order to the state's law and order machinery.

Against Terrorists and Non-State Actors (NSA), following additional aspects should be included in the military strategy:

(a) Military strategy against terrorists and non-state Actors should be fully integrated in the national security strategy formulated to address any form of aggression against the nation's sovereignty and territorial integrity.

(b) Unlike the strategy against Naxals, that against terrorists and NSA would have to take into account particular aspects as follows: -

   (i)   Against terrorists who are Indian nationals.

   (ii) Against foreign terrorists who may or may not be Non-State Actors[3].

---

[2] It relates to bringing normalcy. State of normalcy differs from place to place and should be clearly defined for a given area.

[3] In 1999 the so called 'mujahids' turned out to be regular soldiers of Pakistan Army in the Kargil war.

SUMMARY

Home-grown Solutions

Terrorism is a scourge that has afflicted not only national security but the well-being of all Indian citizens. It is the most important threat of our times. It is not, however, an insurmountable predicament. India has immense know-how of dealing with terrorism and subterfuge. We need to look no further than our own experience for wisdom and solutions. We could, by all means, learn from the knowledge of other nations and the best practices that they have built up from the likes of 9/11 and London bombing but draw lessons from on our own equally devastating traumas. The sagacity that we have inherited from the great Guru of strategy, Chanakya, and honed by our present day statesmen-strategists equips us adequately. After all we have dealt with terrorism longer than any other nation in the world.

Basic Principles

Statesmanship calls for multi-faceted attributes of leadership. The hallmark of good statesmen is their ability to discern between civility and contempt; civility with those that respect law and contempt with others who have only disdain for civilized behaviour. Leadership, in turn, should be guided by strategy.

Since actions of terrorists are based on intimidation, shock and ruthlessness of execution, the military strategy to defeat such tactics must be tailored around three basic principles: -

(a) Prepare and prevent.

(b) Swift and effective retribution

(c) Effective deterrence to the point of creating fear in the minds of NSA and their sponsors.

Tail Piece

Military strategy against terrorism must be a good blend; humane, fair and within the bounds of the law on one hand and realistic, unforgiving and robust on the other. The shield must be forged in the crucible of national pride and the sword unsheathed from time to time to keep the blade sharp, shining and rinsed out in the blood of our enemies.

Crafting a Comprehensive Approach

Ajit Doval

When we talk about strategies, normally we take either of the two approaches, either by design or default. Normally we tend to do by our deductive logic, reasoning, lot of reading, internet downloading, and another is we base it on our empirical experience, what India is what India's neighbourhood is. It makes it very impressive and particularly in seminar to talk about reasoning, deductive logic, quotations, I think I would like to deviate from that and like to be matter of fact on the ground.

When it comes to the question for strategy building for India, there are two distinct aspects, one is as has been mentioned by Gen. Patankar also where the source, the inspiration, the logistics and the strategic goals and objectives are of a foreign adversary that has to be met, we will have to have entirely a different strategy for that. Second, which are our internal fault lines either used by the external forces and the internal forces, how do we deal with that. But there are certain commonalities in dealing with all of them and one of the commonality which I had been hearing and I think you all had been talking about is the lack of political will. Let us examine this because now we are talking it in a strategic context. There is never a lack of political will. There is less of policy options. Political will manifests itself once you provide them that these are the four policy options and we can execute each four of them. You tell us which one you want us to execute. But if you tell them they have got no options or any option they ask you can execute, and you say none, then there is no question of exercising the political will.

Now why do these policy options shift. These policy options are directly proportionate and related to our capacities. For example after Mumbai attack even if the government had the political will to have a covert operation to blow up Lashkar-e-Toiba headquarters and they said okay we have got the political will, we will face the consequences you go and do it. Were the intelligence apparatus or the security apparatus in the country, in a position to accept the challenge. Did we have the precise intelligence, did we have the plan made for that. Did we have the personnel who had rehearsed that, did we have the people on the other side who were going to do it. If you don't have it, the policy options become very clear and this I am telling you because it is not only at the level of the prime minister, this happens at the level of everyone, at your level, at the level below you, and the lower command of that. A large number of times there are many things that you want to do but you are not able to do it. So, this capacity building where policy options can be exercised is an extremely important factor.

The capacity building will have a different form for Pakistan and for internal threat like the left wing extremism. For example about left wing extremism, what do I consider as the biggest cause of anxiety for the country. It is not that 76 CRPF personnel were killed on 6th April. My biggest cause of concern is that on 4th November 2004 the Prime Minister of the country declared that this is the country's biggest internal security threat that the country is facing and we are going to deal with it at a war footing. There cannot be a more powerful statement at that level. In an address to the nation, Prime Minister stated that in last six years, the left wing extremist affected states has gone up from 76 districts affected in 9 states in 2004, to nearly 260 districts in 14 states. Their cadre strength has increased from 7500 to nearly 16000, the killings have gone from 550 to about 1300, their money collection from 40 crores has gone to 1200 crores and their weapon holding has gone from 6500 to 14000. This is immaterial, these statistics mean nothing. What is important is that, if the nation decides to deal with a problem at a war footing and this decision is taken at the highest executive level in the government, is this the capacity that the country can produce? What happens if the problem is bigger. Is it the capacity, is it the strength with which we will be able to secure the future of this country. This is only a illustration. It is not something that I say, of course these figures are not very disturbing that way. 14000 cadres even if they are there, can be dealt with. So, I think the first requirement would be that problem by problem, area by area, issue by issue, we will have to decide what are the appropriate capabilities that we require at the cutting edge level. There is no point in having it at the policy level that we are going to pump in 1400 crore rupees for police modernization. We often start talking about the means as the ends. This 1400 crores in the modernization grant or raising 150 battalions of paramilitary forces. They are means to an end, what is to be achieved, what is the strategy and that strategy has got to be translated right from the broad policy objective to the tactical detail. Unless there is a total connect, it is just like you are producing electricity in Bhakranangal, it won't reach Delhi in case there is a 30-inches of a cut in Ambala. It has got to be the total circuit that is completed and that in Indian conditions normally does not take place.

A good amount of money that has been sent to the left extremist areas for developmental purposes has only increased the financial muscle of the left wing extremists because there was no infrastructure available to absorb it and to execute it. There was no PWD which could go there and make the roads. There were no workers there, and everybody was corrupt on top of that. So, everybody gave the certification that the work has been done. To have development in an area, it is important to create an infrastructure first to channelise the resources. If you want to do the police build up, then you need to first define what you want in the police build up. If you want 150 expert interrogation teams, what all they should have, they should have 150 interrogation centres, they should have tape recorders, they should have videos, they should have whatever the modern aids of interrogation which are required, they should have databanks and then build that up and then work backwards for the money. We get the resources but lack planning in utilisation of these for the purpose for which it is alloted.

The second point which I think has been made is also about the strategy for the civil society. Now this strategy for the civil society is important both in respect of our external and internal threats. In respect of external threats, our civil society is taken as an object of subversion whose minds have to be manipulated to behave and exercise in a way that would help our enemy powers. I think Mr Praveen Swamy talked about the Qurban Ali doctrine. One of the components of the Qurban Ali doctrine was that India is an artificial state and its Balkanisation is a historical inevitability and in that the Muslim population of India will play an important role and Pakistan will be an important stakeholder at that point of time. With that doctrine they would like to do something to continue their propaganda amongst them, use the fundamentalist forces, use some of the radical ideas to be injected amongst them and inside it comes to about the question of say the naxalites propagating the theory of violence, the theory of Marxism through the barrel of a gun and things like that.

Now, who is going to disabuse the minds of the people of this pernicious ideology. In the State how the civil society is going to be insulated from these negative thoughts. This is the responsibility of the political thinkers, of the political workers, of the political parties. It is for them to go from village to village and say that how a totalitarian extremist globally discredited political ideology is counter productive for youth and how democratic or constitutionalism is something which is good for them. This work cannot be done by the policeman. If in the tribal areas the naxalites are carrying out the propaganda, then the government's propaganda machine will neither have the credibility nor it can engage itself in a political argument. If the political parties are able to raise their cadres for manning every booth in an electorate of 1000 people they have got a huge networking and if all the political parties are together they would be able to educate them in the villages, in the far flung areas to tell them by the word of mouth. After all what did Gandhiji do, what were all political movements about. In this battle the principal fight is between that political leadership which believes in constitutionalism and parliamentary democracy and those who want to dispossess them of power and say that we are going to come here through the power of the gun and thereafter going to stay. They are opposed to the police because they stand in the way. They think that police is a coercive organ of the State which is preventing them from seizing that power. So, it is a fight for power and if in this fight for power there is an ideology, the conflict of ideology is also involved and therefore the role of the political leadership becomes extremely important and this point is not fully understood because in whichever areas where we have either failed or succeeded it has been on account to a very large extent of the role played by the policy part.

Now, earlier in almost all internal security problems by and large there was a consensus amongst the ruling and the opposition parties but we find that on left wing extremism and now Islamic radicalism these are the two issues one external and one internal which have got great destabilizing potent for the country and we have not been able to develop a consensus amongst the political parties. The need is firstly they develop the consensus, second they activize their cadres, educate their people, first get themselves convinced that this ideology got these pernicious thoughts, they have to be opposed and certainly the government's information machinery can do many other things. Inform the people about the developmental work, about their right, provide whatever steps that the government has taken all these things but then the political propaganda part of it will have to be countered by the political apparatus.

I think in our strategic response there is a shift to a greater degree required that intelligence capability is to be used or to be developed from an instrument of providing policy inputs or providing intelligence or information for policy inputs as an instrument of policy execution. In this country I think we had for some years probably somewhere in mid-90s deliberately gave up the intelligence agencies role as being instruments of policy execution. Let me try to explain it. I don't say that all intelligence agencies should go because they don't have any legal mandate to do anything and therefore they should start indulging in illegalities. It is not that. For example in our neighbourhood region what is our capability to influence the political thinking there, the thinking of the political leadership there, the different political parties which are there in the fray. When we say we influenced it, it is not necessarily that we are using a coercive method. There are methods of reasons and there are various other methods or whatever it might be. After all the United States is able to influence what is happening in Pakistan or many other countries in the world. India cannot become a global player, a global power player unless it has got the ability to manipulate the developments in its neighbourhood.

Now, manipulation through coercive methods of the State is the last resort which probably army does or the defence forces do but short of that there is a manipulation of events that is through the leadership level interactions, there are summit level interactions, there are political level interactions, there are interactions of the NGOs, there are thinkers and then I think there is a big role that intelligence agencies play and this is also important. For example, when people talk about the left wing extremism in the 70s, what was the strategy to counter it. One of the factors was to divide the left wing extremist movement. All these groups which mushroomed ultimately going up to 94 groups not only having ideological differences and personality clashes but even leading to cross fires amongst them. From Vinod Mishra's time for about 15-20 years the left wing extremist movement became very dormant. Now how they were created and when they are created I don't think that you do any illegal part of it but there were genuine differences, you highlight it there. It is just like the politicians play the political move. Do we understand the politics of it.

Let me say one thing to the credit of the ISI. This is world's one intelligence agency which can take credit for this capability amongst the coercive groups or amongst what we may call as the non state actors. It is able to use them in different roles, even at a great cost to them and still are able to have their control, command and to some extent respect for them. They were able to fight the Taliban, remove them from power, still cultivate them, keep a section with them, make one section fight with the other, call them the soft Taliban and the hard Taliban, try to catapult the soft Taliban into the positions where they could control greater areas, they are able to force Karzai who was their staunch opponent, probably he is still not convinced that Pakistanis are their friends but now he is prepared to go the Pakistani way and not the Indian way. There is the Indian State, even after having them so much in Bangladesh, it has left very few prints. The conditions in Pakistan-occupied-Kashmir are so bad, there had been lot of discontent there but they have been able to manipulate, they have been able to arrest Hafiz Sayeed or Iqbal Cheema or Zarar Shah and still have Lashkar-e-Toiba totally under their control or having taken action in Bhagalpur against Jaish-e-Mohammed people and Azhar Masood and still have control over the organistaion and the leadership. This I am only telling as an example. That is what the capability of having the control over the destabilizing elements at the intelligence level is extremely important. In addition to that the conventional intelligence upgradation at the ground level, I don't think I need to add anything on that because plenty has been said and all of us understand that it is extremely important.

There is one important factor in making a strategy. That Is, whatever adversary whether it is a non-state actor that we have to fight, we have to have a nationally agreed definition, a nationally agreed perception of what the enemy is, not in nebulous adjectival terms but in precise noun terms. It is true that army cannot counter terrorism, it can only catch a terrorist but at the end of it you have to fight only the terrorists. It has got to be in the tangible form. Now, we at times have not been able to accept the ground realities and accept that this constitutes a national danger. If demographic invasion from Bangladesh is not only considered by the Supreme Court as a national danger but has said that the IMDT Act tantamounted to an aggression against the state. There cannot be a bigger indictment against the government in power, that is you are guilty of having committed an aggression in your own country, that is this IMDT Act was an act of aggression. The problem is that we are not prepared to face that this is a problem. This is a problem, we have to face it.

If we think that Left Wing Extremists have taken to the weapons, and they want to destabilize the society. They are only using an excuse of the problems of the tribals, or the caste conflicts in Bihar or the agrarian problems in Andhra or they are telling that they are supporting the secessionist movement in Kashmir or giving the support to the SIMI and IM telling that we stand for Islamic radicals. This is part of the anti-imperialistic strategy, this is all mystifying. This is all something to mislead the people. The fact remains that they are prepared to join hands with everyone who is prepared to bleed India. They stand as an antithesis for Indian nationalism and let us accept it as such. If we accept it as such, then the development factor is a very very important factor. It stands on its own merit but as far as naxalites are concerned they have got to be fought. Same thing is true for Islamic radicals and the jihadis. There is no question of having our negotiations or talks if we have clearly decided that unless the perpetrators of Mumbai massacre are accounted for by Pakistan we cannot hold any negotiations with them. Now we are not only prepared to have negotiations but in fact even talk Kashmir and even water which were never existent. So, this sort of a dichotomy and confusion probably takes us away from having a strategic view.   If we have taken a strategic view that Pakistan considers India as a compulsive enemy and unless Pakistan gives up that or we are not going to use the process of negotiation. Gen Kayani was very right in telling after he returned from Brussels three days before the comprehensive talks at the foreign secretary level were to take place, he said India is our natural and long term enemy. Whether we hold talks with them or fight with them it will be within that framework. This is strategic clarity. They are clear about it that India has got to be treated as an enemy, even if we are talking to them we will talk to extract the best terms by which our relationship of enmity is transacted in a way which is most beneficial to the interest of Pakistan. So, I think the strategy should be based on clarity of objectives, total integration of our long term and short term objectives, should be based on the ground realities as exist and not as you wish them to be and we should take into factor the various components and various resources. If we are not able to put all of them together individually, you will not get the best results while dealing with them.

Veledictory Address

❑ **Admiral Madhvendra Singh, PVSM, AVSM (Retd)**

GOC-in-C South Western Command, Admiral Shekhawat, Generals Officers, Ladies and Gentleman,

Jai Hind and very good afternoon to you all

It has been a very interesting, informative and educational day where we in Jaipur have been fortunate to listen to experts giving their views on a topic of not just of national security interest but of Inter-national security interest.

To the views of this galaxy of experts I must add my own, making clear that they are my own, may be a bit out-dated as one is no longer in the know having been out in the cold for almost six years now and finally I must add that what ever I say is in the Indian context. I have no doubt that other countries have found their own solutions and have a better success rate than we have had.

Having heard the experts' one is left with the firm conviction that there are no easy answers and certainly there is no magic formula or single solution to the problem. All one can say is that for our Campaign against Non-State Actors (NSA's) we have to use all the tools of Statecraft – diplomatic, economic, gentle persuasion, political, and violence.

Frankly, I do not believe that most of these guys are non-state actors. If they were, they would be of little consequence because they are akin to Daku Man Singh –petty criminals or murderers. In a sense every murderer is a non –state actor. But nobody, can have the sanctuaries they have, the funding they have, the training and intelligence they have, the types of weapons and equipment they have – with out state support. Therefore, if we want these so called NSAs to be controlled we must first try and convince, if not control, the State actors concerned, As far as we are concerned all the NSAs are being supported by our neighbour to the West. They may also come from Bangladesh or Nepal or Sri Lanka or from the sea, but the fact is that they originate from Pakistan or are controlled, trained and funded by that country. We have tried everything in the book with Pakistan hoping that they will see reason but to no avail. And we can keep trying but we will get no joy for a variety of reasons which I will not elaborate here-the primary ones that we have no bargaining chip that will force them to see reason and the fact that they do not want friendship with India. The only country that has that power today is the USA and we should ensure that they use their diplomatic/financial/military clout to rein in Pakistan. They also have the power to influence Saudi and all other nations with a surplus of petro-dollars, who are funding these NSAs in the name of religion. One might say that the Maoists of Chattisgarh are true blue NSAs but just the other day 20 Tons of arms and ammunition headed for them were seized in Lucknow. Who is sending them?

The other powers that can influence Pakistan are Russia, China and the European Union. So the first step has to be diplomatic and our diplomatic campaign is bearing fruit to the extent that the world has finally realized what we have been saying at least since the late nineties-that Pakistan is the epicenter of terrorism.

Besides Diplomatic, Political and economic the state can try gentle persuasion. But who should we try and persuade? Is it the terrorist or the terrorist organizations? They have been so deeply indoctrinated that persuading them is out of the question. And sadly they are being indoctrinated in the name of religion. And even more sadly it is the same religion everywhere in whose name these NSAs are acting. There is no point mincing words in a forum like this-that religion is Islam. I am no expert on religion but I am sure no religion encourages its followers to commit the type of terrorist acts that many of these guys are committing in the name of their religion. The problem is not just political or economic. The problem has acquired a religious overtone. You can't reason with religious passions; religion is the opiate of the people, and only wise, mature people of that religion can influence the misguided people of that particular religion. The other day I was asked a direct, but somewhat loaded, question by an American " Do you like the Muslims", To which I said" I like all good Muslims – just as I like all good Hindus, Sikhs or Christians." So we have to request the Good Muslims everywhere to put some sense into these misguided people.

Then comes the political level within the country. Those NSAs with genuine grouses against the country need to be neutralized/placated/won over by political measures-perhaps the best example of this are the Maoists. I have no doubt that they are also receiving support from states inimical to us – but essentially their cause is political in nature and so the GOI and the state governments concerned must have a dialogue with them and redress whatever grievances they have – before the ISI steps in and starts to inflame passions and giving support to make them a powerful NSA which I think they are already doing. Speaking at a seminar on piracy at sea in 2005 I had said "Today's pirate is tomorrows Terrorist". That is already happening. Similarly I would like to add that "todays Maoist is tomorrows terrorist". That too is happening – but before they become true terrorists, we need to do more at the political level and essentially that "more" boils down to economic prosperity – which means development. But can there be development without security? The answer is no. A good example is India – it is because the Indian Armed Forces have given the country peace and security for forty years that the country has developed economically at such a fast rate.

So we come to perhaps the last tool of state craft left- Violence-something which a soft state like India seems to be shying away from. Violence is an instrument of state policy, just as war is an extension of state policy by other means. The question always arises as to what should take precedence – Human rights or National security. I have no doubt in mind – National Security takes precedence and if a few innocent lives have to be sacrificed in the interests of National Security – so be it. Far more people die in road accidents in Jaipur then are killed by security forces in J & K.

We are talking of terrorism today as if it is a new phenomenon. The fact is that it is not. The state was the original terroriser – and this has been so right through history with the Roman Empire.

It is an old saying-to catch a thief set a thief. So to counter Non State actors the state must have its own non state actors, the state must also have its own exterminators. We are in the business of violence. War is all about violence. In war you shoot to kill. And if someone is waging war against the state you should order his killing. I am sure there are enough people and organizations in the country who are capable of doing so.

If somebody can issue a Fatwa to kill someone surely any state has the right to exterminate any one waging war against it. War is legitimate; and if the state orders violence to be used at least it is legitimately authorized. Just as violence is an instrument so is killing an instrument and the state must order the killing of known terrorists and wait for extradition treaties etc.

Now you may say that what I have just said is not morally right. But to that I would reply that morality is a luxury that nation states cannot afford and secondly while it may not be morally right it is the right thing to do.

The last point I would like to make is that it has taken the Maoists or the LeT or JM 30 to 40 years to reach these menacing proportions. We should not expect the problem to be solved in a jiffy or in three months or six months or even a year. We should not be gung ho about it and proclaim to the whole world that we will wipe out so and so with in a particular time frame. That is not going to happen in a hurry but we should not worry because time is always on the side of the state. The state outlives individuals. Wait for the next generation – they will see the benefits of joining the Indian mainstream and the futility of being a permanent fugitive.

Finally, I would like to thank Gen P K Singh , The entire team of USI and all the speakers for making this seminar possible and I would like to thank the GOC-in-C and the South Western Command team for excellent arrangements for the seminar.

Thank You and JAI HIND

www.ingramcontent.com/pod-product-compliance
Lightning Source LLC
Chambersburg PA
CBHW070810300326
41914CB00078B/1927/J